MAO ZEDONG
A Preliminary Reassessment

Stuart R. Schram

The Chinese University Press Hong Kong
St. Martin's Press New York

All rights reserved. For information, write:
St. Martin's Press, Inc., 175 Fifth Avenue, New York, NY 10010
Printed in Hong Kong
First published in the United States of America in 1983
ISBN 0-312-51405-0

Library of Congress Cataloging in Publication Data

Schram, Stuart R.
  Mao Zedong, a preliminary reassessment.

  Includes bibliographical references.
  1. Mao, Tse-tung, 1893-1976.   2. Heads of state—China—Biography.   I. Title
DS778.M3S33 1983   951.05'092'4[B]   83-9173
ISBN 0-312-51405-0

Contents

Contents

Mao Zedong and Mao Zedong Thought Revisited

Byron S. J. Weng

It is generally agreed among observers that Mao Zedong occupies a prominent place in the twentieth-century history of China and that Mao Zedong Thought has had an epochal influence on Chinese politics. However, whether his is a life deserving of praise or culpability, and whether his thought has been a blessing or a curse to the Chinese people, that is a matter still widely disputed. Though his coffin has been nailed shut, the verdict is as yet unclear.

The judgment rendered in the "Resolution" on certain historical problems adopted by the Communist Party of China at the Sixth Plenum of its Eleventh Central Committee in June 1981 was half affirmative and half critical. Mao Zedong Thought was called "a crystallization of the collective wisdom" of the Chinese Communists, although its content was mostly explained by quotations from Mao's various writings. While such a treatment is indeed a more rational and more balanced one when compared to earlier blind and empty acclamations, still the well-informed remain largely unconvinced.

Why is this so? In my view, it is because the "Resolution" carries only political authority, not the power of truth; because a political party may adapt to external conditions by various means, including self reform, in order to secure its own survival and progress, but will not obey truth because it is truth, nor negate itself for the sake of truth; because Mao Zedong and Mao Zedong Thought, inseparable from the CPC as they are, should not, and in fact no longer, belong solely to the CPC; and because there are numerous delayed maladies and latent diseases from the Mao Zedong era whose treatment and cure require more objective analysis and more realistic diagnosis than was given.

In China where the traditional political culture has at best a thin and weak basis for the rule of law, the existence of a benevolent and able ruler has always been of key importance. The pulse of good government goes up or down by virtue of the existence of such a ruler. Even enlightened and sagacious leaders found themselves unable to depart from such a tradition of rule by man. In his time, Mao Zedong organized and led a mammoth peasant revolution to seize power and made himself a supreme national hero and a globally acclaimed leader. So much so that 900 million people's fate was tied

to his person and countless masses of workers, peasants and soldiers wor-
shipped him as god. Even though some pointed to his old age and accused
him of playing god with the lives of China's multitudes, the passing of such a
"great helmsman" surely must cause the Party and the country alike to suffer
a profound uncertainty and loss of direction whether one loves or hates him.

How great must be the task of his successor! How difficult it must be! The
more so when one read of the so-called "Crisis of Belief, Confidence and
Trust" among the people in China. Further we learned, and came to understand, how the "Whateverists" attempted to safeguard their position by
raising the banner of Mao Zedong and how the "pragmatists" had to face,
even after subduing their "Whateverist" rivals, the dilemma of dealing with
the question of Mao's historical status. Mao and Mao Thought can and must
be criticized but cannot and must not be abandoned, they discovered. Indeed,
it is far too early to let Mao's reputation die with him.

Mao Zedong Thought was born during the first half of the twentieth
century in China as necessitated by revolution. It opposed the traditional
metaphysical philosophy of the Confucian school, advocated Marxist-Leninist
socialism, challenged the prevailing fatalistic way of thinking, and gave the
CPC and its Red Army a needed theoretical basis and guiding ideology.
Thanks to it, the much humiliated "sickman of Asia" regained its status and
stood up again to enjoy some respect from the rest of the world. Even though
this Mao Zedong Thought cannot adequately replace the codes, custom and
culture accumulated over thousands of years in China, even though it also
brought great disasters such as the Great Leap Forward and the Cultural
Revolution to the Chinese people, perhaps the time has not yet come for Mao
Zedong Thought to cease having its life and its historical function.

It is precisely because Mao's name and Mao Zedong Thought both have
important utility still that we should not fail to give them serious, objective
and careful scrutiny. Will the recording in history books that Mao's "contributions far outweigh his mistakes" meet the test of truth and time? Will such
an evaluation inadvertently encourage the remnants of "the Gang of Four" or
the zealots of "Politics Take Command" and "To Rebel Is Justified" in later
years? Is Mao Zedong Thought really the right formula for seizing power and
for ruling a country? Will its "peasant socialism" not become an obstacle to
China's modernization? Can its "people's war" theory fulfil China's defense
needs in the nuclear and space age? Is the method of "dividing one into two"
likely to create for China and even the whole world more and more contradictions, struggles and disasters? How much of the dilapidated, pitiful state of
political, economic, social, cultural affairs in the post-GPCR China was attri-
butable to Mao and Mao Thought? What are the merits and demerits of
maintaining Mao's reputation and Mao Zedong Thought? Is China doomed to

another adventure into the "Second Kind of Utopia" such as the people's communes and the world of Red Guards? The questions to be raised are many indeed.

In order to make further inquiries into such questions, the United College of The Chinese University of Hong Kong was able, under the auspices of the Distinguished Visiting Scholar's Lectures Programme newly created in its Jubilee year, to invite Professor Stuart R. Schram to present a series of three special lectures under the general title, "Mao Zedong: A Preliminary Reassessment."

A renowned scholar in his field, Professor Schram is certainly one of the most distinguished specialists on Mao Zedong and Mao Zedong Thought. That he is a diligent and accomplished scholar is well established by the long and impressive list of his publications appended to this volume. Among the many China scholars outside of China, he is one of the few who have displayed a familiarity with pertinent materials seldom matched by others as well as a critical and penetrating insight into his subject matter. No doubt, his ability to use seven languages and his varied and interesting personal background must have been among the factors contributing to his considerable achievement.

Born on 27th February, 1924 in Excelsior, Minnesota, he is an American who has spent a half of his life so far in England and France. He graduated from the University of Minnesota in 1944, magna cum laude, with a major in physics and minors in mathematics and chemistry. From 1944 to 1946, he worked at the "Metallurgical Laboratory," the University of Chicago in military uniform as a member of the Manhattan District, U. S. Army Engineer Corps. As assistant to the Head of the Technical Information Section, he helped develop a system of classification subsequently used by the Atomic Energy Commission for all reports. Fortunately for us, he took steps to change his career plans and entered Columbia University in 1946 to pursue advanced studies in political philosophy and international law and relations. At Columbia, he studied with such intellectual giants as Franz Neumann, John Hazard, Robert MacIver, Philip Moseley and Reinhold Niebuhr.

Professor Schram, however, was not yet a specialist on Chinese affairs in those days. His doctoral dissertation, completed in 1951, had to do with Protestantism and politics in France. From 1951 to 1954, he first lectured on American civilization at the School for Interpreters, Germersheim am Rhein, and then did translations and research on European problems at the European Center of the Carnegie Endowment in Paris. What followed was a long period of association with two distinguished academic institutions, Centre d'Etude des Relations Internationales, Fondation Nationale des Sciences Politiques, Paris, 1954-1968 and the School of Oriental and African Studies, University of London, 1967 to date.

In 1960, Professor Schram became Head of the Chinese and Soviet Section (jointly with Hélène Carrère d'Encausse) of the Centre d'Etude des Relations Internationales and began conducting research on the thought of Mao Zedong in earnest. This new venture took him to Harvard University for post-doctoral work in Chinese studies twice in the early 1960s, to prolonged stays in Japan, Taiwan, Hong Kong, and India during the 1960s and 1970s. Since 1978, he has visited the People's Republic of China a number of times, to engage in conversations with theoreticians such as Liao Gailong 廖蓋隆. In the 1970s, he also served as a visiting Professor in the University of California, Berkeley, Macalester College, St. Paul, Minnesota and in Keio and Kyoto Universities in Japan. At SOAS, since 1967 he has been Professor of Politics with reference to China. From 1968 to 1972, he was concurrently Head of the Contemporary China Institute.

Of his many publications, some ten books deal specifically with contemporary China. *The Political Thought of Mao Tse-tung* has seven or eight translations around the world and was hailed by the respected London *Economist* as "a major piece of scholarship and a penetrating instance of intelligence in the service of analysis." *Mao Tse-tung*, the biography, has been translated into ten languages, while *Marxism and Asia* and *Mao Tse-tung Unrehearsed* have each appeared in four or five languages. Numerous other articles published in several languages in leading international journals have also been received as authoritative works.

From 13th to 26th April, 1982, Professor Stuart R. Schram was a resident Distinguished Visiting Scholar at the United College. In that period, he generously shared his time and expertise with the students and staff of the United College as well as those of the other Colleges of The Chinese University of Hong Kong and of the larger Hong Kong community through formal and informal receptions and a seminar, in addition to delivering the three featured lectures. His talk at the seminar with staff will be published shortly in substantially revised form in a volume eidted by Dr. J. L. Watson. (For details see Appendix B.)

Those of us who were privileged to hear Professor Schram's lectures are happy to see this special volume published so that others may also benefit from his analyses and insights. Mao Zedong and Mao Zedong Thought will be with us for some time to come yet, and we trust that Professor Stuart Schram will continue to shed new light on this important subject in the years ahead. Allow me to conclude this introduction now by noting our appreciation to Professor Schram for his significant contribution and to all those who have helped for their cooperation and support in this fine event.

Preface

As indicated in Dr. Byron Weng's Introduction, this volume contains the text of the lectures which I had the privilege of delivering in April 1982 at United College, together with substantial extracts from the transcript of the discussions which took place following each lecture. In any case, I should not have wished the book to appear without some expression of gratitude on my part to my hosts at the college for the honour they did me and the kindness they showed me on this occasion. But I have also been impelled to write this brief preface by the desire to explain some minor variations between the text published here and the lectures actually delivered, and more broadly, the relation between this "preliminary reassessment" and the ongoing re-examination of Mao Zedong's life and thought in which I have been engaged in recent years.

It was announced in the press at the time of my visit to Hong Kong that I would be going directly from United College to the Institute of Marxism-Leninism Mao Zedong Thought of the Chinese Academy of Social Sciences for a period of research in the context of the exchange agreement between the Chinese Academy of Social Sciences and the British Academy. In the end, I spent a total of approximately six weeks, in April-May and September 1982, mainly in Beijing, but also in Nanjing and Shanghai. Shortly after my arrival in April, Liao Gailong, then Deputy Director of the Institute of Marxism-Leninism Mao Zedong Thought, asked for a copy of the lectures I had given in Hong Kong, and he subsequently commented on this manuscript in very considerable detail. We were not, of course, able to agree on everything, and neither he, nor any of my other Chinese interlocutors, bears any responsibility whatsoever for the opinions I have expressed here. In certain cases, however, I took his views into account in revising the text, and this should be noted briefly.

First of all, I must agree that, from 1925 or 1927 onwards, Mao was more than a simple apprentice, and I have therefore changed the title of the first lecture from "The Apprenticeship of a Revolutionary" to "The Formative Years." Secondly, I have accepted Professor Liao's correction on a point of fact, namely that Deng Tuo 鄧拓 was not beaten to death in May 1966 (as suggested by one account in the Chinese press which I followed in my lecture), but rather committed suicide. Beyond this, I have rewritten the passage in the third lecture about Mao's propensity to wreak vengeance on those who had crossed him so as to express my view on this delicate question with greater precision. No doubt these two paragraphs, as they stand in this volume, would still be regarded in Beijing as too harsh, but in any case I hope I have eliminated any misunderstandings which might have resulted from too loose and sweeping a formulation.

Thirdly, I have corrected the statement, in the third lecture, that "Mao Zedong Thought" is now used simply as a synonym for Marxism as correctly applied in China. Not only Liao Gailong, but several other scholars, pointed out to me that, apart from Mao's own works (or such of them as are still regarded as correct), the term "Mao Zedong Thought" is currently employed to designate only such good and useful works by Liu Shaoqi, Zhou Enlai, and others as deal with themes which Mao himself at least evoked or sketched out, and not with aspects of Marxism completely absent from his own writings.

Speaking more generally, my two visits to China in 1982 provided, in addition to the opportunity to read a number of unusual source materials, great intellectual stimulation from the extended conversations, amounting to approximately 100 hours in all, which I had with Liao Gailong, Su Shaozhi 蘇紹智(Director of the Institute of Marxism-Leninism Mao Zedong Thought since May 1982), and many other responsible theoretical workers. In the light of the new ideas and new information derived not only from these exchanges, and from contacts with scholars in Hong Kong and Japan on my way to and from China, but from reading the increasingly wide range of published materials now available, I have continued, during the past year to develop my interpretation of Mao Zedong Thought, and of other theoretical problems of the Chinese revolution.

In particular, I have written the first draft of a chapter on Mao's thought from 1949 to 1976 for Volume 15 of the *Cambridge History of China*. The first half of the lectures published here was derived in substantial part from an abridgement of my chapter on Mao's thought to 1949 for Volume 13 of the *Cambridge History*, completed earlier. (I take this opportunity to thank Professor John K. Fairbank, the editor of the *Cambridge History of China*, for permission to draw on this material here.) In the case of the post-1949 period, the relationship was the other way round: the relevant portion of the lectures I delivered at United College constituted a preliminary sketch for the much more detailed text I have now written.

Since this volume commemorates an occasion which took place in April 1982, it did not seem appropriate to revise the treatment of Mao's thought in the 1950s and 1960s to incorporate wholly new themes and insights which were not even mentioned at that time, nor shall I list such topics here. The point I want to make in this connection is rather that, although I shall in future be having new things to say about Mao Zedong and his Thought, in broad outline the interpretation I put forward in the course of my attempt at a "preliminary reassessment" last year still corresponds to my position. I hope that readers will find this concise overview of some interest.

Stuart R. Shram
20 June, 1983

MAO ZEDONG
A Preliminary Reassessment

I

The Formative Years, 1917-1937

In this and the two following lectures, I propose to offer an interpretation of Mao Zedong's 毛澤東 thought, and of his contribution to the Chinese revolution. I have called this a "preliminary reassessment" because I think that is what can reasonably be attempted at the present time. Five years ago, I contributed to a volume called *Mao Tse-tung in the Scales of History.* Speaking not of my own essay, but of the work as a whole, I would say this was not a bad book, considering that it was written only six months after Mao's death. But the title was, to put it mildly, a presumptuous one. History had not rendered its verdict, and could not have rendered its verdict on a figure of such magnitude in so short a time.

In a sense, no verdict on a man who changed either the course of events, or accepted patterns of thought (and Mao changed both) can ever be called final. Many such individuals are re-evaluated, and argued about, decades or even centuries after their disappearance. Circumstances do make possible today, however, a more informed and serious assessment of Mao's role than in 1977. On the one hand, the Chinese themselves have begun to come to terms with Mao's heritage, by winnowing through both his ideological contributions, and the political and economic realities he left behind him in an effort to distinguish positive from negative aspects. Apart from taking advantage of the ideas and information thrown up by this process of re-examination within China, outside observers have also had time to reflect, and to distance themselves from the obsession with the Cultural Revolution which prevailed during Mao's last years.

It will probably be another three to five years at least before we are able to achieve sufficient perspective to formulate a judgment which begins to approach what may be the longer-term verdict regarding Mao Zedong's contribution to the Chinese revolution. But I think we have now reached a first plateau from which to survey the ground and put forward a preliminary synthesis.

One question immediately suggests itself: why should I, who was born in Minnesota, a very long distance both culturally and geographically from China, come here to Hong Kong and offer such a reassessment to an audience composed in substantial part of people who are themselves Chinese? As many of you will know, this is not a purely rhetorical question, for there was considerable resentment a decade or so ago, in certain circles here in Hong Kong, that an ignorant foreigner such as myself should dare to analyse and to judge the work of China's Chairman. These sentiments were, of course, greatly exacerbated by the political climate of the Cultural Revolution decade, and some of those involved may well see things differently now. There is, however, not only a political but a cultural dimension to this problem, and one which cannot be lightly brushed aside.

The point is that an essential aspect of Mao Zedong's search for a revolutionary theory adequate to China's needs, and more broadly of the process of change which has been under way for a century and more, is the problem of cross-cultural borrowing. And because of the vitality and cohesion of Chinese thought and society even in a period of relative decline, this phenomenon has taken on in China a somewhat different guise from that observable in many other Asian and African countries following the Western impact. Although Tan Sitong 譚嗣同 raised the slogan of "wholesale Westernization," and many other writers subsequently called for the elimination of key aspects of traditional Chinese culture, and above all of Confucian influences, an absolute break with the national past was never in fact a practical possibility. What took place was rather the incorporation of ideas of foreign origin into a context which remained intrinsically Chinese.

Mao himself, while he sought in that peculiar Westernizing ideology known as Marxism-Leninism the ideas and methods by which to re-shape his own society, also stressed the need to adapt and transform Marxism in the Chinese environment. Indeed, he went so far as to assert, in Yan'an 延安 days, the continuing validity of certain aspects of the Chinese tradition of statecraft; and even when, as was frequently the case, his attitude was hostile to tradition, it is impossible properly to understand the new and radical ideas he put forward without an awareness of what he was reacting against. Moreover, in his last years, as everyone knows, Mao Zedong turned increasingly to the heritage of the Chinese past, not only for his own reading pleasure, but as the source and justification for current policies.

It is therefore extremely difficult to do any kind of justice either to Mao's life or to the Chinese revolution unless one can move easily back and forth between ideas of European origin and the realm of Chinese culture. That is something few foreigners can achieve, and I do not claim to be one of them. None the less, I have persisted, during the last twenty years or so, in my efforts to understand the cultural dimension of China's twentieth-century transformation, as well as its political and social dimensions, because of the great intrinsic interest of the subject, and the significance for the world as a whole of this particular instance of interaction between East and West. And I have come here to Hong Kong, in response to the kind invitation of United College, to share my ideas with you, because I believe these problems are too complex to be fully apprehended from any one point of view, and should be the subject of a dialogue between "insiders" and "outsiders."

It is, incidentally, only because you *are* insiders that I shall be able to deal, in only three lectures, with so vast a topic as the development of Mao's ideas during a period of nearly sixty years. Knowing that the basic facts, both of Chinese history and of Mao's own life, are thoroughly familiar to you, I shall focus on those episodes which I regard as of greatest significance, or about which I have something new to say, evoking other aspects of Mao's career only briefly, to provide the necessary continuity.

Let me turn, then, to the topic of this first lecture: the evolution of Mao Zedong's political thinking from young manhood to the beginning of the Anti-Japanese War. In terms both of age and experience, Mao was a member of the May 4th generation. An avid reader of *Xin qingnian* 新青年 from the time of its first appearance in 1915, he served his apprenticeship in political organization and in the study of politics under the influence of the "new thought" tide, and his career as a revolutionary effectively began in the wake of the May 4th demonstrations.

Mao Zedong's political views prior to his early twenties are known only from odd fragments of contemporary documentation, and from his own recollections and those of others many years afterward. He first emerges clearly into our field of vision with an article, entitled "A Study of Physical Education," written when he was approximately twenty-three, and published in the April 1917 issue of *Xin qingnian*. The overriding concern—one might almost say obsession—which runs through the whole of this article is anxiety lest the Chinese people should suffer the catastrophe of *wang-guo* 亡國, that is, of losing their state and becoming "slaves without a country." "Our nation is wanting in strength," he wrote. "The military spirit has not been encouraged. . . . If our bodies are not strong, we will be afraid as soon as we see enemy soldiers, and then how can we attain our goals and make ourselves respected?"[1]

Mao thus evoked at one stroke two basic themes of his thought and action throughout the whole of his subsequent career: nationalism, or patriotism, and admiration for the martial spirit. But if Mao is clearly preoccupied here with what might loosely be called nationalist goals, was his nationalism at this time conservative or revolutionary? An obvious touchstone for deciding this

[1] "Ershiba hua sheng" 二十八畫生 [Mao Zedong], "Tiyu zhi yanjiu" 體育之研究, *Xin qingnian* Vol. 3, no. 2, 1917; passage translated in S. Schram, *The Political Thought of Mao Tse-tung*, revised edition (New York: Praeger, 1969), p. 153.

point is whether or not he saw the aim of *fu-qiang* 富强 as in any way tied
to a social and cultural revolution perceived as a necessary precondition for
strengthening the nation. In fact, the article shows us a Mao concerned with
China's fate, but almost totally uninterested in reform, let alone revolution.
And yet, though there are no explicit references to social change, the article
does contain definite signs of modern and non-conformist thinking. One
theme which revealed unmistakably modern influences, was that of the
importance of self-awareness (*zijue* 自覺) and individual initiative (*zidong*
自動). Mao put the point forcefully at the beginning of the article:

> Strength depends on drill, and drill depends on self-awareness. . . . If we wish to
> make physical education effective we must influence people's subjective attitudes
> and stimulate them to become conscious of physical education. . . .[2]

Although the idea that the key to effective action lies in transforming the
hearts of men can be found in the Confucian tradition, the main inspiration
for passages such as this is to be found in the eclectic, but basically Westernizing ideas Mao had absorbed from his reading of *Xin qingnian*, and from the
lessons of his ethics teacher and future father-in-law Yang Changji 楊昌濟. In
a letter to Yang, written probably in 1917, he expressed himself however, in
favour of drawing on Chinese as well as on Western sources in developing
ideas adapted to current reality. "In my opinion," he wrote, "Western thought
is not necessarily all correct either; many parts of it should be transformed at
the same time as Oriental thought."[3] This repudiation of radical Westernization in favour of a synthesis between Chinese and foreign ideas was also to
characterize Mao Zedong in after years.

Like Yang, he laid particular stress on the role of the will. But at the same
time, in very Chinese fashion, he regarded an authentic will as impossible
without understanding, or enlightenment. In the letter of 1917 to Yang
Changji just cited, he went on to say:

> . . . truly to establish the will is not so easy; one must first study philosophy and
> ethics, in order to establish a standard for one's own words and actions, and set
> this up as a goal for the future.

But it was not merely a matter of subjective attitudes; action and commit-
ment were required:

> Then one must choose a cause compatible with this goal, and devote all one's
> efforts to pursuing it; only if one achieves this goal, is it possible to speak of
> having [a firm] will. . . .

---

[2] *Loc. cit.*
[3] "Gei Yang Huaizhong xiansheng de xin" 給楊懷中先生的信 (Letter to Mr. Yang
Huaizhong [Changji]), *Ziliao xuanbian* 資料選編 (n.p., January 1967), pp. 10-11.

Mao's thinking evolved very rapidly during his last two years at the First Normal School in Changsha 長沙. Perhaps the most important single element which makes its appearance in 1917-1918 is an explicit and strongly-marked individualism. For example, in marginal annotations to a textbook on ethics by the German neo-Kantian, Friedrich Paulsen, Mao wrote:

> The goal of the human race lies in the realization of the self, and that is all (*renlei zhi mudi zai shixian ziwo eryi* 人類之目的在實現自我而已). What I mean by the realization of the self consists in developing our physical and mental capacities to the highest degree.... Wherever there is repression of the individual, ... there can be no greater crime. That is why our country's "three bonds" must go, and why they constitute, with religion, capitalists, and autocracy, the four evil demons of the realm.... [4]

Like older and more eminent intellectuals of the time, such as Chen Duxiu 陳獨秀, Li Dazhao 李大釗, or Lu Xun 魯迅, Mao had seized on the notion of the absolute value of the individual as a weapon to combat the traditional insistence on the absolute value of authority and precedent, and thereby to "break out of the nets" of the old culture and the old society.

By the time he had returned to Changsha in the summer of 1919, following a visit to Beijing during the winter of 1918-1919, and been drawn into the experience of the May 4th Movement in Hunan, Mao had changed in many respects very considerably as compared to 1917 or even 1918. And yet, the fact that he was learning rapidly about the theory and practice of revolution did not mean that he had been converted to Marxism, or had much understanding of it. Indeed, in the three-part article he contributed to the journal he edited in Changsha in July and August 1919, the *Xiangjiang pinglun* 湘江 評論, under the title "The Great Union of the Popular Masses," he compared Marx with Kropotkin, concluding that the ideas of the latter were "broader and more far-reaching."[5] If this article has a discernible philosophical bias, it is to be found perhaps less in socialism, or in anarchism, than in the ideas of

---

[4] Quoted by Li Rui 李銳, *Mao Zedong de zaoqi geming huodong* 毛澤東的早期革命活動 (Changsha: Hunan Renmin Chubanshe, 1980), p. 110. This biography of the young Mao (originally published in 1957 under the title *Mao Zedong tongzhi de chuqi geming huodong* 毛澤東同志的初期革命活動) is the fullest account available in any language of his life and thought down to the mid-1920s. The first edition has been translated into English: *The Early Revolutionary Activities of Comrade Mao Tse-tung*, translated by Anthony W. Sariti, edited by James C. Hsiung, Introduction by Stuart R. Schram (White Plains, New York: M. E. Sharpe, 1977). This quotation appears on p. 38 of the translation, but the striking first sentence is missing; generally speaking, the original edition is less well documented, and above all considerably more hagiographic, than that published in 1980.

[5] Mao Zedong, "Minzhong de da lianhe" 民眾的大聯合, *Xiangjiang pinglun*, nos. 2, 3, and 4, 1919. I have published a full translation of this text: Mao Tse-tung, "The Great Union of the Popular Masses," followed by S. Schram, "From the 'Great Union of the Popular Masses' to the 'Great Alliance'," *The China Quarterly*, no. 49, January-March

Western liberalism, as transmitted by Yan Fu 嚴復, Liang Qichao 梁啓超, and Yang Changji—and also by Hu Shi 胡適.

In his editorial for the first issue of the magazine, Mao said, after enumerating the progress in various domains which had been achieved by humanity since the Renaissance (for example, from a dead classical literature for the aristocracy to a modern, living literature for the common people, and from the politics of dictatorship to the politics of parliamentarianism), that in the field of thought or philosophy, "we have moved forward to pragmatism."[6] I do not mean to suggest, in noting this point, that Mao was a disciple of Hu Shi or John Dewey. His favourable evaluation of pragmatism in 1919 did reflect, however, an attitude he was to maintain *almost* until the end of his life, to the effect that one should not spin theories without linking them to concrete experience.

If Mao's ideas in 1919, like those of older and more learned men at the time, were thus a mosaic of many influences, his article "The Great Union of the Popular Masses" had one remarkable peculiarity: it represented one of the few attempts to put forward a general programme on the basis of concrete experience of the revolutionary mass movements of the May 4th period. It is true that Mao's hierarchy of social categories was quite un-Marxist: he attributed maximum importance to the student movement, and relatively little to the peasants, not to mention the workers. He also, characteristically, devoted considerable attention to women, and to school teachers. The central theme of the article is that China's renewal will come above all from the rebellion of young people, and especially of students, against the old order.

Although Mao showed little understanding of Marxism at this time, his imagination had been caught by the victory of the Russian revolution. He listed the establishment of a Soviet government of the workers and peasants first among the world-wide exploits of what he called the "army of the red flag," and went on to mention the Hungarian revolution, and the wave of strikes in America and in various European countries. The numerous other articles written by Mao for *Xiangjiang pinglun* likewise convey his sympathy for those who were denounced as "extremists," including not only the Bolsheviks, but Rosa Luxemburg. But they also express very strong support for the Germans, who are presented as an oppressed people dictated to by the Entente.

The idea of China as a proletarian nation, which should show solidarity

1972, pp. 76-105. The passage about Marx and Kropotkin occurs on pp. 78-79 of the translation.

  [6]Mao Zedong, "Fakanci" 發刊詞, *Xiangjiang pinglun*, no. 1, 1919; translated in M. Henri Day, *Máo Zédōng 1917-1927*. Documents (Skriftserien för Orientaliska Studier nr. 14, Stockholm, 1975), p. 81. (For the reasons for translating *shiyan zhuyi* 實驗主義 as "pragmatism" see Day, p. 83, note 2.)

with other oppressed peoples, was of course commonly put forward in the years immediately after the May 4th period, by Li Dazhao, Cai Hesen 蔡和森 and others. Mao, too, was naturally drawn in this direction. Broadly speaking, the overall impression of his political outlook conveyed by the article "The Great Union of the Popular Masses" is that he favoured spontaneous (but not unorganized) rebellion by the popular masses against all forms of oppression, whether by the domestic power-holders or by the foreign imperialists, and did not much discriminate between various ideologies as long as the movements of liberation they inspired were genuine and effective.

A phase in Mao's subsequent apprenticeship which provides a highly suggestive complement to his analysis, in 1919, of the role of grassroots organizations in social change was his participation in the Hunanese autonomy movement in the following year. The record of this episode throws a revealing light not only on Mao's intense Hunanese patriotism, but on his attitude to political work generally. In an article published in September 1920, he wrote:

> In any matter whatsoever, if there is a "theory," but no "movement" to carry it through, the aim of this theory cannot be realized. . . .
>   I believe that there are two kinds of real movements: one involves entering into the midst of things [ru yu qi zhong 入於其中] to engage in concrete construction; the other is set up outside, to promote [the cause].

Both types of movement, he added, were and would remain important and necessary. At the same time, he stressed that an effective movement must have its origins in the "people" [min 民]. "If this present Hunanese autonomist movement were to be successfully established, but if its source were to reside not in the 'people,' but outside the 'people,' then I venture to assert that such a movement could not last long."[7]

By putting the term "people" in quotation marks, in the sentence I have just read, Mao himself underscored its ambiguity. Were these the "popular masses" [minzhong 民衆] of his 1919 article? Or were they the "Chinese people" or "Chinese nation" [Zhonghua minzu 中華民族], who were never far from the centre of his concerns? It is perhaps a characteristic trait of Mao's thought that these two entities are indissolubly linked. He was never, at any time after 1918 or 1919, a nationalist solely, or primarily, interested in China's "wealth and power." But neither was he a "proletarian revolutionary"

[7] These materials—four articles by Mao, and a proposal for a constitutional convention drafted jointly with two others, were discovered by Angus McDonald in the course of research on his doctoral dissertation, now published as a book, The Urban Origins of Rural Revolution (Berkeley: The University of California Press, 1978); he has published the Chinese texts in Hōgaku kenkyu, Vol. 46, no. 2 (1972), pp. 99-107, with a commentary in Japanese. See also his article in The China Quarterly, no. 68, December 1976, pp. 751-777. The passage quoted here appears on p. 99 of Hōgaku kenkyu.

like M. N. Roy, who never thought in terms of the nation. Mao's writings and actions during the first period in the history of the Chinese Communist Party, from 1921 to 1927, clearly demonstrate the linkage, in his thinking, between "masses" and "nation."

Mao's experience during these six eventful years falls neatly into three segments. During the first two years, he was engaged in organizing the labour movement in Hunan, and this could be called his workers' period. Thereafter, in 1923-1924, he served as a member of the Chinese Communist Party's Central Committee, and of the Shanghai Executive Bureau of the Guomindang 國民黨, in Canton and Shanghai, and this could be called his period as an "organization man." Finally, as everyone knows, he devoted himself in 1925-1927 largely to organizing the peasant movement, and this could be called his peasant period.

The writings of Mao's workers' period are few in number, and largely lacking in the fire and eloquence which Mao, on other occasions, showed himself so capable of manifesting. The main explanation lies, in my opinion, in the fact that Mao himself had never really lived the life of a worker, as he had lived both the life of a peasant and the life of a student and city-based intellectual. He had, to be sure, organized a night-school for workers when he was a student at the Normal School in Changsha, and befriended individual workers on many occasions. His instinctive understanding of their problems was not, however, quite the same. This by no means implies that Mao's experience of the workers' movement was unimportant. His work in organizing strikes in a variety of industries undoubtedly influenced his intellectual and political development as a whole, but at the time the harvest was meagre.

The materials for the years 1923-1925, though by no means abundant are considerably more substantial than those for the previous period. The most important and most controversial of these items is his article of July 1923, entitled "The Peking *Coup d'Etat* and the Merchants." In it, he declared:

> The present political problem in China is none other than the problem of a national revolution [*guomin geming* 國民革命]. To use the strength of the people [*guomin*] to overthrow the militarists, and also to overthrow the foreign imperialists with whom the militarists are in collusion to accomplish their treasonable acts, is the historic mission of the Chinese people. This revolution is the task of the people as a whole, and the merchants, workers, peasants, students and teachers should all come forward to take on the responsibility for a portion of the revolutionary work. Historical necessity and present realities dictate, however, that the work for which the merchants must take responsibility . . . is both more urgent and more important than the work the rest of the people should take upon themselves. . . .

> The broader the organization of the merchants, the greater will be their . . .
> ability to lead the people of the whole country, and the more rapid the success
> of the revolution![8]

When I first published extracts from this text in *The Political Thought of
Mao Tse-tung* nearly twenty years ago, I was, I must confess, moved to some
extent by a spirit of mischief, as well as by the desire to set the record straight
regarding Mao's "firm" class stance at the time. But Mao's views of 1923 also
have positive significance as a bench-mark against which to measure the
epochmaking shift in his outlook which took place two or three years later.
This becomes clear if we take proper note of the argument he employed to
justify the attribution of the leading role in the Chinese revolution to the
merchants. "The politics of semi-colonial China," he wrote, "is characterized
by the fact that the militarists and foreign powers have banded together to
impose a two-fold oppression. . . . The people of the whole country obviously
suffer profoundly under this . . . oppression. Nevertheless, it must be acknowledged that the merchants are the ones who feels these sufferings most
acutely and most urgently." In other words, Mao regarded the merchants,
and more broadly the city-dwellers directly exposed to imperialist oppression, as most capable of playing a leading role in the national revolution
because they suffered the most. This whole sociological analysis was turned
right around three years later, after Mao had discovered the revolutionary
potential inherent in the peasantry.

Following his sojourn in Shanghai, as a member of the Shanghai Executive
Bureau of the Guomindang, Mao returned in the autumn of 1924 to Hunan
for a rest, and began his practical apprenticeship in organizing the peasants.
When he came back to Canton, in the autumn of 1925, to take *de facto* charge
of the Guomindang Propaganda Department, edit *Zhengzhi zhoubao* 政治周
報, begin lecturing at the Peasant Movement Training Institute (which he was
to head from May to October 1926), and participate in the Second Congress
of the Guomindang, he had come to hold the view, from which he was never
afterward to waver, that the centre of gravity of China's revolution lay with
the peasants in the countryside.

In his article of February 1926 on the classes in Chinese society, Mao, while
stressing the numerical importance of the peasantry, and the degree of privation
—and therefore of sympathy for the revolution—prevailing in the countryside,
also characterized the urban proletariat as the "main force" in the revolution.[9]

[8]Mao Zedong, "Beijing zhengbian yu shangren" 北京政變與商人, *Xiangdao* 嚮導, no.
31/32 (11 July, 1923), pp. 233-234. Translated in S. Schram, *The Political Thought of
Mao Tse-tung*, pp. 206-209.
[9]Mao Zedong, "Zhongguo shehui ge jieji de fenxi" 中國社會各階級的分析, original
text reproduced in Takeuchi Minoru 竹內實 (ed.), *Mao Zedong ji* 毛澤東集, Vol. 1 (Tokyo:

Thus, even though the concept of "proletarian hegemony" was inserted in this text only in 1951, he did recognize in early 1926 the Marxist axiom that the workers would play the central role in the revolutionary process. In September 1926, he allowed himself to be carried away by enthusiasm for the revolutionary forces which had been unleashed in the countryside to such a point that he turned the axiom of working-class leadership explicitly on its head.

"The greatest adversary of revolution in an economically backward semi-colony," he wrote, "is the feudal-patriarchal class (the landlord class) in the villages." It was on this "feudal landlord class" that the foreign imperialists relied to support their exploitation of the peasantry; the warlords could be overthrown only by mobilizing the peasantry to destroy the foundations of their rule. "The Chinese revolution," he wrote, "has only this form, and no other."

Not only did Mao Zedong assert the importance of the rural forces of reaction in the old society, and of the rural revolutionary forces in over-throwing them—he went on to argue against the importance of the cities:

> There are those who say that the rampant savagery exercised by the compradors in the cities is altogether comparable to the rampant savagery of the landlord class in the countryside, and that the two should be put on the same plane. It is true that there is rampant savagery, but it is not true that it is of the same order. In the whole country, the areas where the compradors are concentrated include only a certain number of places such as Hong Kong, Canton, Shanghai, Hankow, Tientsin, Dairen, etc., on the sea coast and the rivers. It is not comparable to the domain of the landlord class, which extends to every province, every *xian* 縣, and every village of the whole country.
> ... Hence, although we are aware that the workers, students, and big and small merchants in the cities should arise and strike fiercely at the comprador class, and directly resist imperialism, and although we know that the progressive working class, especially, is the leader of all the revolutionary classes, yet if the peasants do not arise and fight in the villages to overthrow the privileges of the feudal-patriarchal landlord class the power of the warlords and of imperialism can never be hurled down root and branch.[10]

Despite the ritual reference to the "leading role" of the working class, the implication of this passage is clearly that the real centre of power of the old society is to be found in the countryside, and the real blows must therefore be struck in the countryside. In the conclusion to the article, Mao spelled out in startlingly explicit fashion the view that, while the workers in the cities were seeking only limited advantages such as freedom of association, the

---

Hokubōsha 北望社 , 1972), pp. 161-174. The sentence quoted is translated in S. Schram, *The Political Thought of Mao Tse-tung*, p. 247.

[10]Mao Zedong, "Guomin geming yu nongmin yundong" 國民革命與農民運動, *Mao Zedong ji*, Vol. 1, pp. 176-178.

peasants were pursuing no less an objective than the immediate overthrow of the political power of the landlords, which had for so long been crushing them.

Never afterwards was Mao to go so far in explicitly putting the peasants in the place of the workers as the conscious vanguard of the revolution. His Hunan peasant report of February 1927 attributed to the poor peasants the leading role in the struggle in the countryside; it did not downgrade the importance of the cities, and of the classes based in the cities, in the same graphic terms. Nevertheless, the sociological analysis set forth in September 1926 plainly remained at the heart of his thought and action from that time forward.

I have said nothing, in the foregoing account of Mao's activities and ideas in 1923-1927, of the framework in which these activities took place, namely the united front between the Chinese Communist Party and the Guomindang, in the singular form of the so-called "bloc within," involving the entry of Communists into the latter party as individual members. This pattern of collaboration, which was imposed on the Chinese Communists against their will by the Comintern envoy Sneevliet, with the backing of Moscow, has been the object of intense controversy ever since its inception. I shall not go into this whole problem here because however important and intriguing the formula of the "bloc within," Mao played no part in devising it, and contributed nothing at the time to its justification in theoretical terms.

The only comment I wish to make about the framework of the first united front, before turning to the next phase in Mao's career, is that he was able to work effectively in this context because he attached primary importance, in the mid-1920s, to national unification and China's struggle to throw off the domination of the imperialists, and accepted that, for the moment, the Guomindang and its army could provide the only effective spearhed for such a campaign. Such recognition (shared also by Stalin and by Chen Duxiu) of the *de facto* leading role of the bourgeoisie and its party in the Chinese revolution at the present stage, obviously had something to do with Mao's statements of 1923 hailing the contribution of the merchants to the revolution. Even in 1926, when he had begun to mobilize the peasants and to become conscious of their revolutionary potential, Mao was still inclined to believe that there could and should be a place for such dynamic support from below in the overall strategy of the united front. In 1927, on the other hand, having lost all hope that Chiang Kaishek 蔣介石, or even the so-called "Left Guomindang," would support action by the peasants which went dead against their own class interests, Mao Zedong was one of the very first to call for a radical break with these former allies, and for the raising of the red flag in the countryside.

The twenty-year period in Mao's life and thought which I am discussing in this first lecture is split into two exactly equal halves by the dramatic events of the spring and summer of 1927, when the alliance with the Guomindang collapsed in blood, and the massacres carried out in Shanghai on Chiang Kaishek's orders inflicted a blow on the workers' movement in China from which it was never really to recover before 1949. Chiang's action, and the reaction of the Communists to it, led to a decisive change both in the pattern of revolutionary activity under the leadership of the Chinese Communist Party, and in Mao Zedong's own role.

The ensuing two decades were spent by Mao Zedong almost wholly in a rural environment, and witnessed the emergence and triumph of a strategy of "surrounding the cities from the countryside." In one sense, this strategic orientation marked the continuation and development of the ideas Mao had formulated in 1926 and 1927 regarding the role of the peasants in the revolution. But these twenty-two years were also characterized by the existence of two interrelated phenomena which radically modified the political and social context in which Mao henceforth elaborated his ideas: guerrilla warfare as the primary form of struggle against the Guomindang, and base areas as the centre and locus of such struggle.

Apart from the intrinsic interest of his military theories, Mao's involvement in armed struggle left an imprint on his approach to politics in general. While it did not make of him, as some people have argued, a thug who delighted in naked military force for its own sake, it did unquestionably strengthen the emphasis on courage, firmness of heart, and the martial spirit which is visible in his first published article, and never left him until the end of his life.

Secondly, the pattern during these years was not merely one of guerrilla warfare, but of warfare centred on base areas. As Mao himself pointed out in later years, the differences between the Chinese and Soviet revolutions lay not merely in the fact that the Chinese Communists had engaged in armed struggle in the countryside, but in the experience gained by Mao and his comrades in the exercise of effective political control over varying but sometimes considerable areas and populations, long before the actual conquest of power. Thus the Chinese Communist Party stood in a three-fold relationship to the people: that of a revolutionary army, or party in arms, seeking to draw from the "ocean" of the masses the sustenance necessary to the conduct of its operations; that of the "vanguard Party," seeking to carry out a historic mission on behalf of an urban proletariat with which it had very largely lost contact; and that of a government or state within a state, in which capacity it established with the population under its control a complex network of interactions.

As you all know, Mao Zedong set up his first base on the Jinggangshan 井岡山 in early 1928, with the support of Zhu De 朱德 and others, and began trying to develop the contacts with the population without which the campaigns of the Red Army would become merely a military adventure. The environment in which he made this first attempt was a singularly backward and isolated one, and the human material with which Mao had to work was made up largely not of peasants (still less of workers), but of rural vagabonds or *"youmin* 遊民 " who had hitherto been members of two bandit gangs with whose chiefs Mao was obliged to ally himself in order to survive. It is not surprising, therefore, that Mao should have written, in November 1928, in a report to the Central Committee, that his activities on the Jingangshan would remain merely a localized adventure as long as there was no revolutionary "high tide" in the country as a whole.[11]

Early in 1929, Mao Zedong and Zhu De came down from this mountain backwater into a region of Jiangxi province 江西 still relatively poor and backward, but socially somewhat more differentiated, and which included a certain number of market towns. Here Mao may well have felt that he had arrived in a place to which the letter of Marxist formulations could have some relevance. Nevertheless, there remained a very clear psychological and political gulf between Mao on the one hand, and figures like Li Lisan 李立三 and (after Li's fall) the "Returned Students" on the other. And of course, standing above any and all of the rival factions in the Chinese Communist Party was the International in Moscow.

Here it is necessary to say something about the vexed question of the "Li Lisan Line" implemented in 1930. In recent years, attempts have been made to replace the earlier view according to which Li had simply been made a scapegoat for Stalin's blunders by a new interpretation arguing that Li Lisan really was perceived at the time by Moscow as a leftist heretic, and Moscow's man was none other than Mao himself. In my opinion, both these contrasting interpretations are somewhat one-sided. In this context, I cannot examine in detail all the arguments and counter-arguments, but will simply state concisely my own view of this matter. Four crucial issues are: the role of the workers and the peasants; the significance of the Red Army and of the Soviet areas; the time scale of the revolution; and the place of China in the world revolution.[12]

The need for working-class hegemony was, for Moscow, an axiom which could not be challenged without calling into question the whole ideological basis of Marxism-Leninism, as well as the relevance to China of the Soviet

[11] *Mao Zedong ji*, Vol. 2, p. 59; translated in S. Schram, *Mao Tse-tung* (Harmondsworth: Penguin, 1967), p. 136.

[12] For references, and a fuller account of these issues, see my introduction to S. Schram (ed.), *Authority, Participation and Cultural Change in China* (Cambridge: Cambridge University Press, 1973), pp. 9-14.

example. On this issue, the International therefore stood very close indeed to Li Lisan. As regarded, on the other hand, the problem of whether, in the conditions prevailing in China, the Red Army and the base areas in the countryside could play a significant role in the revolution, Stalin accepted sooner and more wholeheartedly than Li the view that the Soviet areas did have an independent role to play, though in early 1930, Li Lisan himself came to see the Red Army as a very useful auxiliary force which could support the action of the workers.

As for the time scale of the revolution, Li Lisan began to entertain, in January-February 1930, extreme chiliastic hopes of immediate victory in the whole country which were regarded in Moscow as altogether utopian, and led to an effort to rein in his enthusiasm. This does not mean, however, that the Comintern had already elaborated, in 1930, as claimed by some authors, what was to become Mao's ultimate strategy of a long-term struggle based on encircling the cities from rural base areas. For in the very directive of June 1930 to the Chinese Communist Party aimed at damping down Li Lisan's excessive enthusiasm, Moscow stated that the revolutionary situation, even if it could not embrace the entire territory of China, "will cover several important provinces . . . in the very near future."[13]

Indeed, Mao himself, though not attaching so much importance to the major industrial centres as Li Lisan, or even Moscow, was by no means bent, in 1928-1930, on pursuing a purely rural revolutionary strategy. As early as April 1929, he put forward a plan for the conquest of the whole of Jiangxi province, including Nanchang 南昌 and other cities, within one year. And in a letter of January 1930 to Lin Biao 林彪, while recognizing that the time limit of one year had been mechanical, he reaffirmed his belief in the possibility of rapid victory in all of Jiangxi, adding that this would be "unthinkable" unless a nation-wide revolutionary high tide were imminent.[14] And once he found himself plunged into action in the summer of 1930, Mao too, like Li Lisan, was gripped with enthusiasm. On 7 October, 1930, as his armies halted at Ji'an 吉安 in their retreat from Changsha, Mao endorsed a resolution declaring that "in the course of this revolutionary high tide . . . soviet power undoubtedly burst upon the scene in the whole country and in the whole world."[15] Thus he manifested not only his hopes of rapid victory, but his conviction that it was China which would light the torch of world revolution.

Despite the failure of his armies to take and hold Changsha, Mao Zedong

---

[13]Translated in H. Carrère d'Encausse and S. Schram, *Marxism and Asia* (London: Allan Lane the Penguin Press, 1969), p. 244.

[14]*Mao Zedong ji*, Vol. 2, p. 139.

[15]Qu Qiubai 瞿秋白, article in *Shi hua* 實話 (*True Words*) (Shanghai), no. 2, 9 December, 1930, pp. 3-4.

survived the events of autumn 1930 with his power and prestige substantially intact. But on this occasion his main rival, Li Lisan, had not enjoyed the full backing of Moscow, not only because some of his policies were seen there as heretical and extreme, but even more importantly because Stalin's preferred candidates for the top positions in the Chinese Communist hierarchy were men such as Wang Ming 王明 (Chen Shaoyu 陳紹禹), Bo Gu 博古 (Qin Bangxian 秦邦憲), and Lo Fu 洛甫 (Zhang Wentian 張聞天) who had been trained at Sun Yatsen University in Moscow, and had been sent back to China in the spring of 1930 specifically to place their first-hand knowledge of Soviet thinking (and their personal loyalty to Stalin) at the service of the Party.

At the end of 1930, their mentor, the Soviet sinologist Pavel Mif, arrived in China to take direct charge of the process of installing a new leadership and setting the Chinese Communist Party on the correct course. The Fourth Plenum of February 1931, presided over and tightly controlled by Mif, put them firmly in the saddle. Henceforth, throughout the remainder of the Jiangxi period, Mao Zedong would find himself in opposition with these men, trained in Moscow and enjoying the direct backing of the Comintern.

Let me take up now some important aspects of Mao Zedong's thought, as it developed before, during, and after the period from 1932 to 1934, when the Moscow-oriented faction effectively imposed their will on him and to some extent reduced him to silence. My first topic will be the problem of the relation between objective and subjective change in the revolutionary process as conceived by Mao.

We have seen that, as early as 1917, Mao Zedong laid great stress on the importance of subjective attitudes, seeing them as the key to changing the behaviour of individuals and groups. In the peculiar circumstances which prevailed on the Jinggangshan, Mao carried this emphasis on subjective factors farther than he had ever done before, suggesting that by changing a person's thinking, it was possible to modify his objective class nature. Discussing the problem raised by the fact that the greater part of his small Red Army was made up not of workers, or even of proper peasants, but of rural vagabonds or éléments déclassés, Mao wrote in his report of 25 November, 1928:

> The contingent of éléments déclassés should be replaced by peasants and workers, but these are not available now. . . .
>   The éléments déclassés are after all especially good fighters. Moreover, casualties are mounting high. Consequently, not only can we not diminish the éléments déclassés now in our ranks, but it is even difficult to find more for reinforcements. In these circumstances, the only method is to intensify political training, so as to effect a qualitative change in these elements.[16]

---

[16]*Mao Zedong ji*, Vol. 2, p. 37; translated in S. Schram, *The Political Thought of Mao Tse-tung*, pp. 268-269.

The same persistent emphasis on consciousness, and even on moral character, as attributes defining man's nature can be traced in the Gutian 古田 Resolution of 1929, where Mao enunciates five qualifications for new Party members, of which only one relates to class (and that to "class consciousness"), the other criteria being purely moral.[17] Looking ahead, incidentally, this approach manifested itself in the definition of the "five-bad elements," coined by Mao in the mid-1950s and still in use at his death, which joyfully mixed sociological categories (landlords and rich peasants), political categories (counter-revolutionaries and rightists), and moral categories (bad elements).

While Mao thus believed that objective social realities could be modified by changes in consciousness, he also saw participation in revolutionary action as one of the most effective means for changing men's thinking. Indeed, an acute awareness of the interdependence between the subjective and the objective, and the deliberate manipulation of this dialectic, was one of the hallmarks of Mao Zedong's thought, and one of the secrets of his political success.

The concept of revolutionary struggle as an instrument for promoting cultural revolution was formulated by Mao as early as 1927, in his Hunan peasant report, where he wrote:

> The abolition of the clan system, of superstitions, and of one-sided notions of chastity will follow as a natural consequence of victory in the political and economic struggles. . . . The idols should be removed by the peasants themselves. . . .[18]

In other words, having educated themselves (or, to use the modern Western jargon, "raised their consciousness") in concrete revolutionary struggles, the peasants would discover the irrelevance of their previous beliefs in the supernatural, and discard them. Incidentally, the reference to "one-sided notions of chastity," i.e. to the demand for chastity on the part of women, but not on the part of men, reflects the continuing interest on Mao's part in the problem of women's liberation which he had eloquently expressed in 1919, and which he continued to manifest at least until the activities of Jiang Qing 江青 during his last years caused him to have second thoughts.

Mao applied his insights regarding the interaction between the subjective and the objective not only to the socio-economic struggles of the peasantry, but also and especially to the military domain.

In his letter of January 1930 to Lin Biao, he criticized Lin for "overestimating the importance of objective forces and under-estimating the importance of subjective forces."[19] By "objective forces," Mao meant in

[17]*Mao Zedong ji*, Vol. 2, p. 95.

[18]*Ibid.*, Vol. 1, pp. 237-238; translated in S. Schram, *The Political Thought of Mao Tse-tung*, p. 259.

[19]*Mao Zedong ji*, Vol. 2, p. 130.

particular the white armies, which were outside the Communists' direct
control, whereas "subjective forces" referred to the Red Army, which they
perceived from inside, and whose motivation and strategy they therefore
understood. But it is plain that he was also talking about objective factors in
the broader sense of objective historical circumstances, and subjective factors
in the sense of the human capacity to influence those circumstances by
"conscious action."

This element in Mao's thinking had been, as I suggested earlier, reinforced
by the context of military struggle in which he developed his ideas and undertook to make revolution from 1927 onwards. Mao saw war as the highest
manifestation of "conscious action" and the supreme test of the human
spirit. He put the point as follows in a passage which he liked so much that he
repeated it in almost identical words in 1936 and 1938:

> Conscious activity is a distinctive characteristic of man, especially of man at war.
> This characteristic is manifested in all of man's acts, but nowhere more strongly
> than in war. Victory or defeat in a war is decided on the one hand by the military,
> political, economic and geographical conditions, by the character of the war, and
> by international support on both sides. But it is not decided by these alone. . . .
> To decide the issue, subjective efforts must be added, efforts in directing and
> waging the war, i.e. conscious activity in war.
> People who direct a war cannot strive for victories beyond the limit allowed
> by the objective conditions, but within that limit they can and must strive actively
> for victory. The stage of action for these directors of war must be built upon
> objective conditions, but on this stage, they can direct the performance of many
> living dramas, full of sound and colour, of power and grandeur. . . .[20]

This passage eloquently expresses what I have called Mao Zedong's
"military romanticism," born out of the experience of many years of bitter
struggle for survival. It would, however, be a gross over-simplification to
interpret Mao's faith in the limitless capacities of man, and especially of the
Chinese people, solely in terms of his own temperament, or of his life of
combat. His emphasis on subjective factors corresponded also, as I have
already suggested, to the necessities of revolution in a transitional society
made up of many disparate elements.

It is this aspect of Chinese reality which provides the link between the
military and political dimensions of Mao's thought and experience. Just as the
outcome of a battle can rarely be predicted with certainty, but depends in
part, as Mao stressed in the passage just quoted, on subjective factors such as
the courage of the soldiers and the tactical skill of the commanders, so the
terms of the political combat appeared less clearly defined in China than in

[20]*Ibid.*, Vol. 6, pp. 99–100; translated in S. Schram, *The Political Thought of Mao
Tse-tung*, pp. 284–285.

Western Europe or even in the former Russian Empire.

On the one hand, the classes and strata which made up Chinese society were far more disparate and difficult to define with precision than was the case in the West. On the other, the behaviour of these different social categories was significantly modified by the impact of the foreign presence.

In the early 1930s, Mao's position regarding the relation between national contradictions and social contradictions was the mirror image of Chiang Kaishek's "unify before resisting." Just as Chiang claimed he could not fight Japan until he had disposed of the "Communist Bandits," so Mao asserted, in a letter of 25 September, 1931, that only the Red Army could resist imperialism and really defend the people, so that the overthrow of the "fucking Guomindang government" [*Guomindang de diao zhengfu* 國民黨的 鳥政府] was the necessary first step to national salvation.[21]

A change in Mao's outlook regarding collaboration with other political forces was signalled by a declaration of 10 January, 1933, which offered, on certain conditions (cessation of attacks on the Soviet regions, granting of democratic rights, and arming of the masses against Japan) to conclude an agreement with "any armed force," i.e. with any dissident commander prepared to deal with the Communists.[22] Although this position still remained within the framework of the "united front from below," laid down in the line of the Comintern, that is to say, an alliance with the supporters of other political movements, rather than with their leaders, the willingness to deal with high-ranking officers of the Guomindang (though not with Chiang Kaishek himself) marked a significant step toward the "united front from above" which was to be set up in 1937.

Nevertheless, while Mao and his comrades in China thus took the first halting steps toward a second united front, they were far more reticent about going all the way than their comrades in Moscow, and the declaration of 1 August, 1935 calling for a united front was in fact issued on behalf of the Chinese Communist Party by Wang Ming, in the context of the Seventh Comintern Congress. It is necessary here to distinguish clearly between basic theoretical or tactical questions on the one hand, and attitudes toward Chiang Kaishek and the Guomindang leadership on the other. With Chiang, whom they knew as the butcher of their comrades and perceived as a traitor to the revolution, they found it very difficult to co-operate, and only agreed to do so under strong pressure from Moscow, in the wake of the Sian affair 西安事變.

Nationalism as an idea and a political force, and nationalists or patriots other than Chiang, they found it, on the other hand, very easy to fit into

[21]*Mao Zedong ji*, Vol. 3, p. 14; translated in S. Schram, *The Political Thought of Mao Tse-tung*, p. 219.
[22]*Mao Zedong ji*, Vol. 3, p. 184.

their scheme of things. In the proclamation on the northward march of the Red Army to fight Japan which he signed on 15 July, together with Zhu De, Mao called once again for a "national revolutionary war," and an alliance with those willing to wage such a war, while striving to overthrow the "band of traitors of the Guomindang."[23] By the end of 1935, as his force re-grouped in December in Wayaopao 瓦窰堡, Mao was prepared to co-operate not only with the "national bourgeoisie," but with those sectors of the capitalist class who were linked to European and American imperialism, and were therefore prepared to oppose "Japanese imperialism and its running dogs." With their support, the "workers' and peasants' republic" would be changed into a "Government of National Defence."[24]

The subsequent conclusion of a renewed alliance with the old enemy Chiang Kaishek himself, and Mao's theoretical response to these changed circumstances, will be one of the topics discussed in my next lecture. Meanwhile, to round off this account of Mao's intellectual development down to the eve of the "Second United Front," I shall say a few words about Mao's début as a Marxist philosopher.

While Mao Zedong had occasionally touched on philosophical questions in his writings of the 1920s and 1930s, it was in the winter of 1936-1937 that he first undertook the serious study of Marxist philosophy. Edgar Snow has recorded how Mao interrupted the interviews which were to form the basis for his "Autobiography," in order to devour a pile of Soviet works on philosophy in Chinese translation which had just reached the Communist capital of Baoan 寶安. Having read these, Mao proceeded almost immediately to deliver a series of lectures on dialectical materialism, of which the works now known as "On Practice" and "On Contradiction" were originally the concluding sections.

Only "On Practice" and "On Contradiction" have, of course, been officially published in China since 1949, respectively in 1950 and 1952. The contemporary evidence that Mao did in fact deliver a course of lectures on dialectical materialism in 1937 is, however, conclusive and irrefutable. It is therefore of some moment that, when asked about the matter by Edgar Snow in 1965, Mao denied authorship of *On Dialectical Materialism.*[25]

The reasons for Mao's sensitivity in this particular case are not far to seek.

[23]*Ibid.*, Vol. 4, p. 364; translated in S. Schram, *The Political Thought of Mao Tsetung,* pp. 220-221.

[24]Report of 27 December, 1935, *Selected Works,* I, pp. 153-178. The term used in the *Selected Works* is "people's government"; I am assuming that Mao originally spoke in 1935, like the Central Committee resolution of two days earlier (*Mao Zedong ji,* Vol. 5, pp. 26-28) of a Government of National Defense.

[25]Edgar Snow, *The Long Revolution* (London: Hutchinson, 1973), pp. 194-195.

A reputation as a Marxist theoretician and philosopher has been regarded, since Lenin's day, as one of the indispensable qualifications for leadership within the Communist movement. It was no doubt with the aim of establishing his credentials in this respect (as Stalin had sought to do before him) that Mao had originally delivered these lectures. It soon became apparent, however, that Mao's lectures on dialectical materialism did not effectively serve their purpose. In very large part, they amounted (especially in the early sections) to unashamed plagiarism of his Soviet sources, and where Mao had expressed himself in his own words, the result was often very crude.[26]

In the context of the recently-promulgated view that Mao Zedong was a man subject to human error, and that "Mao Zedong Thought" was not his creation alone, both the fact that Mao did indeed lecture on dialectical materialism in 1937, and his debt to other authors, especially to Ai Siqi 艾思奇, have now been officially placed on record in China.[27]

I shall not analyse here Mao's lectures as a whole, but this episode provides valuable background for evaluating the two essays that did become an integral part of "Mao Zedong Thought." The first point to be made is that the portions of the lectures corresponding to "On Practice" and "On Contradiction" are notably more original and more interesting than the earlier part of the work. Moreover, while epistemology was often dealt with at some length in writings and translations from Soviet works to which Mao was exposed in 1936-1937, and often came (like "On Practice") relatively near the end of one-volume surveys of Marxist philosophy, the prominence given by Mao to the subject of contradictions was without parallel in any of his potential sources.

Many reasons could no doubt be given for this. One of them flows naturally from the interpretation of his thought already sketched in this lecture. He was, as I have stressed throughout, acutely aware of the complex and ambiguous character of Chinese society (in other words, of the contradictions within it), and sought to incorporate these insights into his revolutionary tactics.

Some idea of the importance attached by Mao to contradictions can be gained from the fact that Chapter 3 ("Materialist dialectics") of his lecture notes runs to 53 out of a total of 100 pages of *Dialectical Materialism*.[28]

[26] On Mao's plagiarism, see the note in my article "Mao Tse-tung and the theory of the permanent revolution, 1958-1969," *The China Quarterly*, April-June 1971, pp. 223-224; also K. A. Wittfogel, "Some remarks on Mao's handling of concepts and problems of dialectics," *Studies on Soviet Thought*, III, no. 4 (December 1963), pp. 251-277.

[27] See the materials in *Zhongguo zhexue* 中國哲學, Vol. 1 (n.p., 1979), pp. 1-44.

[28] This figure corresponds to the only complete edition of Mao's lecture available outside China: *Bianzheng weiwulun* 辯證唯物論 (Dalian 大連: Dazhong shudian 大衆書店, n.d. [probably c. 1946]). The proportions would, of course, be the same in any printing.

Why was this portion of the lectures so much superior to the earlier sections? In essence, I think because Mao was dealing not only with notions which appealed to him, but with their concrete application to the circumstances of the Chinese revolution. The first chapter of *Dialectical Materialism* was, on the other hand, in large part simply a summary of the history of philosophy in Greece and the West, as perceived by Soviet authors. Here Mao could only copy his sources, and was in no position to add anything of himself.

It was often been argued, and up to a point the claim is accepted even by Cohen, that Mao's most notable contribution to the science of dialectics lay in his elaboration of the concepts "principal contradiction" and "principal aspect of the principal contradiction." I should like to suggest, to begin with, that Mao's use of these categories can be linked directly to his subtle understanding of Chinese reality. A Marxist revolutionary in a society of the type observed by Marx himself, which was perceived as increasingly polarized into capitalists and proletarians, should have been in no doubt as to which were the basic contradictions between classes, or between the productive forces and the mode of production. In broad terms, this pattern was expected to remain more or less the same until the conflict was resolved by revolution. In China, on the other hand, where neither the internal situation nor relations with foreign powers were stable or predictable, it was not merely an intriguing intellectual problem, but a pressing tactical necessity, to determine which factor, or contradiction, was crucial or dominant at a given time.

It is interesting to note that one of the earliest Soviet writings translated in China, a volume published in Shanghai in 1933, devoted a section to the "leading" [*zhudao* 主導] aspect of contradictions, but stated that this was in general always *the same*: for example, in the contradiction between base and superstructure, the base was always dominant.[29] This is one of the points in Mao's essay which Cohen finds most significant; he draws attention to the passage which reads:

> Some people think that . . . in the contradiction between the productive forces and the relations of production, the productive forces are the leading aspect; in the contradiction between theory and practice, practice is the leading aspect; in the contradiction between the economic foundation and its superstructure, the economic foundation is the leading aspect, and that there is no change in their respective positions. . . . True, the productive forces, practice, and the economic foundation generally manifest themselves as the leading and decisive factors. . . . But at times, such aspects as the relations of production, theory and the superstructure in turn manifest themselves as the leading or decisive factors;

---

[29] Li Da 李達 (translator), *Bianzhengfa weiwulun jiaocheng* 辯證法唯物論教程 (by Xiluokefu 西洛可夫 and others) (Shanghai: Bigengtang shudian 筆耕堂書店, 15 May, 1933), p. 295.

this must also be admitted. When the productive forces cannot be developed unless the relations of production are changed, the change in the relations of production plays the leading and decisive role. . . . When the superstructure—politics, culture, and so on—hinders the development of the economic foundation, political and cultural reforms become the leading and decisive factors. . . .[30]

Cohen makes of this passage one of the key links in his argument that Mao did not write "On Contradiction" in 1937; Mao could not possibly, he says, have gone against Marxist "determinism" in this fashion until Stalin had shown him the way, with his writings of 1938 and 1950.[31] The facts speak otherwise. There are some variants in this passage (between the original version and that of the *Selected Works*) but with the exception of the replacement of *zhudao* 主導 (leading) by *zhuyao* 主要 (principal), Mao made no major changes in 1952 in those portions which I have actually quoted here. It would seem that Mao derived his "voluntarism" directly from the study of Lenin (to whom the term was, after all, first applied), and also from his own personality, and the experience of the Chinese revolution.

One final point about Mao as a philosopher concerns precisely his debt to Stalin. The current version of "On Contradiction" has a long and fulsome passage about Stalin's analysis of the peculiarities of the Russian revolution as a "model in understanding the particularity and universality of contradiction." This turns out to have been completely absent from the original version, where Mao illustrates his point rather by the exegesis of a quotation from Su Dongpo 蘇東坡, who is said to have thoroughly understood the relation between the universal and the relative.[32]

Chapter 2 of *Dialectical Materialism* contains the statement that, because the "dialectical materialist currents developing in China today do not result from taking over and reforming our own philosophical heritage, but from the study of Marxism-Leninism," we must "liquidate the philosophical heritage of ancient China," which reflected the "backwardness of China's social development."[33] This statement would appear to have been the product of a momentary feeling of intimidation on Mao's first exposure to Marxist philosophy. It certainly does not correspond to his view, over the remaining four decades of his life, regarding the problem of cultural borrowing. Mao's allusion to Su Dongpo as an authority on dialectics was, in fact, a better guide to the direction in which his thinking would subsequently develop, in the context of the War of Resistance against Japan.

[30] *Bianzheng weiwulun*, p. 93.
[31] Arthur Cohen, *The Communism of Mao Tse-tung* (Chicago: University of Chicago Press, 1964), pp. 23-24.
[32] *Bianzheng weiwulun*, p. 86.
[33] *Mao Zedong ji*, Vol. 6, p. 275; translated in S. Schram, *The Political Thought of Mao Tse-tung*, p. 186.

Questions and Answers

Dr. Byron Weng: Thank you, Professor Schram. There are many fine points in your lecture that we would want to digest before we can engage in a meaningful discussion with you. Today we do have in the audience several learned scholars. Some are authorities on the historical periods of the 1920s and 30s in China and some are authorities on the later periods of revolution. Perhaps they can lead us toward a dialogue with some questions.

Q. Could you elaborate further on some of the main issues during the 1933 to 1934 period that were so frustrating to Mao?

A. The Twenty-Eight Bolsheviks, having taken control of the party in early 1931, then proceeded in the summer and autumn of 1931 to come to the base area. Progressively, Mao was pushed more and more to one side. During the first two years, from 1931 to 1933, he controlled at least the State apparatus. He lost control of the army to Zhou Enlai 周恩來 during the summer of 1932. At this time Zhou was working on the side of the Twenty-Eight Bolsheviks—the Moscow-oriented faction, but Mao did control the government. After 1932 Mao did not control the army, and after January 1934 he didn't control anything. He was reduced, from January 1934 onward, to the role of a figurehead—the figurehead chairman of the Soviet Republic. He was probably under house arrest in the summer of 1934 before the beginning of the Long March. Thus, even when Mao made a speech as Chairman of the Soviet Republic, we do not know whether he was really expressing his own views.

One place where we can see Mao's own hand, his own mind at work is the land investigation movement, the so-called *chatian yundong* 查田運動. Trygve Lötveit concludes that during the first phase of the land investigation movement, in 1933, Mao ran it, and from January 1934 onwards it was the Twenty-Eight Bolsheviks who took over control of everything, including the state. They ran it and pushed it much further to the left. When Mao was in charge of the movement, the philosophy of the land investigation movement and the approach to social change behind it were similar to those behind land reform subsequently. It used the same mass mobilization, the same mass meetings to denounce the landlords, speak bitterness (*su ku* 訴苦) and so on. The land investigation movement was supposed to be a movement to discover whether land reform had been correctly carried out, and everyone had gotten his fair share. In fact, it was primarily a movement with a political thrust, aimed at ferreting out the landlords and the rich peasants. Mao said in one of his speeches of 1933 during the land investigation movement, "*Shuo ye shi tamen hui shuo, xie ye shi tamen hui xie*" (說也是他們會說，寫也是他們會寫). This is a reference to the landlords and rich peasants, who were both more articulate and literate than the other peasants. Due to this and their social prestige some of them crept back into positions of influence, e.g., as chairman of peasant associations. The purpose of the land investigation drive was really to root out these "big tigers."

Here I think we can see Mao's approach to social change at work in the sense that it is only when the peasant has confronted the landlord face to face and shouted him down and in some cases sent him off to be shot or otherwise disposed of, that the peasant feels that something has changed and that he is the master of the new society. This is one interesting ideological element in the Jiangxi period.

Q. During the period between 1917 and 1937 do you think Mao was more a nationalist than a communist, or the other way around?

A. No, I don't think he was more a nationalist than a communist during this period as a whole. There is plenty of nationalism from beginning to end, a virulent nationalism, or patriotism if you happen to regard nationalism as a pejorative term. In 1917 he was an old-fashioned nationalist—so old-fashioned that he referred in an article to Zeng Guofan 曾國藩 as Zeng Wenzheng 曾文正, demonstrating a respect not to be seen later. In 1919 Mao was an ardent Chinese patriot like everybody else, including Li Dazhao. In 1919, Mao, Li Dazhao and others were relatively confused about Marxism, but by the late twenties and the thirties, as we move into the Jiangxi period and on into the Yan'an period I do not think it is right to refer to Mao as primarily a nationalist. He was a revolutionary who was also deeply attached to his own people. There could be no socialist future for China unless there was some kind of future for China; therefore China had to be defended against Japanese aggression, but that doesn't mean that Mao put nationalist goals first. In 1938 he quite obviously put national goals first and said that the Guomindang was the leader and the backbone of the Chinese revolution and that Mr. Chiang Kaishek was the leader of the whole nation. He was capable of subordinating communist goals to nationalist goals under particular circumstances, but that doesn't mean that he was essentially a nationalist and didn't have a communist idea in his head.

Q. In 1980 Wang Ming published a book in Hong Kong arguing that before 1949 Mao had read only one third of Marx and Engels' works, and prior to the beginning of the Sino-Japanese War only about one third of Marx and Engel's works had ever been translated into Chinese. Mao did not

know a foreign language. Having heard this argument do you still think
he was more communist than nationalist?

A. I do not think that argument has any weight. It is perfectly true that
Mao, unlike Wang Ming, had not been to the Soviet Union, and could not
read Lenin in Russian. Unlike Zhou Enlai and others he had not been to
France and learnt to read Marxist writings in French, English and
German. But if somebody has read only a few basic things like the
Communist Manifesto and a few writings of Lenin—and Mao had read a
bit more than that—and is resolved to make a social revolution, taking
these theories as his guide, then one may call him in some sense a Marxist.
It is possible to argue that Mao was a crude Marxist, or didn't understand
Marxism very well, but that is not decisive as to whether his motivation
was to make social revolution, or whether he was simply a Chinese
nationalist.

Q. Are there any signs of influence from Trotsky on Mao's ideology?

A. Well, I see no signs of influence on Mao at that time. Of course, there was
some Troskyist influence in China, and Chen Duxiu and others eventually
turned to Trotskyism. In 1958, Mao put forward a theory of "permanent
revolution," and because of this the Soviets have called him a Trotskyite.
They have also called him an anarchist, a petit bourgeois peasant revolutionary, and all sorts of things. Personally, I think that there were more
differences than similarities between Mao and Trotsky, as is illustrated by
a comparison of their respective theories of the permanent revolution.
That point I will take up in my third lecture.

As for the twenties or even the thirties, Mao took a negative view of
Trotsky, and identified Trotsky with the Li Lisan line at that time. Mao
was not influenced by Trotsky for two reasons. First, Mao had read
relatively little Marx and Lenin, and there was even less opportunity for
him to read about Trotsky in the 1920s, especially up on the Jinggangshan.
He went to the Jinggangshan to make peasant revolution with the lumpen
proletariat or éléments déclassés, or bandits or whatever you want to call
them, and one cannot imagine a more un-Trotskyist thing to do. If there
is one essential trait of Trotsky, it is his emphasis on the European
working class or the urban proletariat. There is no indication whatsoever
of the influence of Trotskyism on Mao in the 1930s. There is some on
the communist movement in general, but on Mao, no.

Q. In the early phases of the revolution, did Mao show any strong inclination
that literature should be at the service of the revolution?

A. Generally speaking, I do not have the impression that he thought very
much or wrote very much about literature. He was more concerned with
concrete problems, such as organizing the revolution in the cities and in

the countryside. He functioned as a journalist in Changsha in the early twenties at the same time that he was involved in the workers' movement. But I cannot imagine that literature as a political force was an important aspect of his thought.

In the early and mid-thirties there were many people in Shanghai and elsewhere sympathetic to the communists. Mao was out in the countryside, at times not in control of his own government or even his own movement, and was not in a position to appreciate very much what these people thought and said. From 1937 onwards the picture is completely different, and there are all kinds of people from literary and artistic circles, such as Ding Ling 丁玲, active in the Communist movement.

Q. Did Mao refer to the intellectuals during the period prior to 1937?

A. Of course, he referred to them all the time, during the May Fourth period because that is what he was, basically. He explained subsequently that although born a peasant, he had turned away from his peasant origins and regarded workers and peasants as dirty, and intellectuals as clean. He really did not turn back to the countryside and re-discover the peasants until 1925. For a full decade, roughly from 1915 to 1925, he spent most of his time in the cities consorting with intellectuals and to some extent, with workers. In 1919, he attributed a greater role to students and intellectuals in his article, "The Great Union of the Popular Masses." His views then were a bit like the philosophy of the New Left in the United States or Europe in 1968 or 1970: students are going to create a new world, and it is the students who are in a sense the vanguard of the revolution.

In 1921 Mao started the self-study university, Zixiu Daxue 自修大學, and had continuing contacts with intellectuals. During the period in 1925 to 1926, when he was working in Guangzhou, teaching and lecturing at the Peasant Movement Training Institute, he also lectured at the Political Training Institute and had contact with people at Huangpu Military Academy. But once he went to the country in 1927, for the next decade, he was fighting for his life. There were hardly any workers there, and fewer intellectuals. Just a few in the party. So intellectuals did not loom large in his scheme of things during that decade. Thereafter, when the December Ninth Movement of 1935 got off the ground, then the students came back into Mao's field of vision, and were important to him again. The support of sympathetic leftists and liberal intellectuals became very important to him.

Q. Is there any evidence in Mao's thought of an attempt to use traditional Confucian ways to build a utopia? Is there any connection between these ideals?

A. I would say, yes, there is some connection, though we can perhaps more usefully take up the question after the second and third lectures. For example, Mao allowed to be used, in the Chinese translation of an interview with Agnes Smedley, the term *da tong* 大同 as a symbol for communism. This text of 1937 referred to *guoji datong yundong* 國際大同運動, meaning, the World Communist Movement. Many of you are better qualified than I to say if this is a Confucian notion, for this is a Chinese, and not a Western notion. Liu Shaoqi was, of course, accused of being a Confucian gentleman back during the Cultural Revolution, but Mao's thought also overlapped with Confucianism, namely in his emphasis on moral self-cultivation, on virtue, as a necessary element of knowledge. But to the extent that there are Confucian utopias, I suppose that they are rather para- or quasi-Confucian utopias held by the peasantry. In the early period, Mao was more concerned with modernizing China's outlook than with maining tradition. He was still under the influence of the May Fourth Movement, and its call to "Overthrow the Confucian family shop" (*Dadao Kongjia puzi* 打倒孔家鋪子).

A Quarter Century of Achievement, 1937-1962

The word "revolution" has two basic meanings. On the one hand, it evokes a fundamental change in the locus of power in society, usually carried out by violent or extra-legal means, in which certain social categories, and/or political movements, seize control of state power from others. But the term is also used to designate the radical re-structuring of society and the economy carried out by the revolutionaries once they have successfully seized power.

I have called this lecture "A Quarter Century of Achievement," and as you will have noted from the dates, the quarter century in question falls almost equally on the two sides of the great divide of 1949. In other words, it was achievement both in overthrowing the Guomindang, and in socialist trans-formation. The title is *not* meant to imply that Mao's contribution during each of these two twelve-year periods was identical in nature, or even of the same importance. As you know, his leadership from 1957 to 1962 is regarded today in China as erratic, to say the very least, and on the whole I share that judgement. Nevertheless, I *do* wish to argue that Mao Zedong made significant contributions to the theory and practice of revolution both before and after the conquest of power, and that there are elements of continuity which run through the whole of the years from 1937 to 1962.

In looking first at the development of Mao's ideas prior to the establish-ment of the Chinese People's Republic, I shall focus successively on three themes: (1) changing relations between various social classes, and the problem of who should lead the revolution, in the context of the Anti-Japanese War; (2) what Mao called the "Sinification of Marxism," and its implications for relations between the Chinese Communist Party and Moscow; and (3) methods of leadership, evoked by the slogan of the "mass line."

As background to the discussion of Mao Zedong's views regarding the role of the different classes in the revolution in the late 1930s, I propose to summarize briefly his interpretation of Chinese history at this time. The most systematic statement on this topic is to be found in the first chapter of *The Chinese Revolution and the Chinese Communist Party*, published in December 1939. (Although Mao himself actually wrote only the second chapter, he did choose to include the whole in his *Selected Works*, and thereby took responsibility for the contents.)

To begin with, the transition from slave-holding society to feudalism was placed here at the beginning of the Zhou dynasty, or roughly in the eleventh century B.C.:

> [China's] feudal society, beginning with the Zhou 周 and Qin 秦 dynasties, lasted about 3,000 years. . . .
> . . . It was the feudal landlord state which protected this system of feudal exploitation. While the feudal state was torn apart into rival principalities under the Zhou, it became an autocratic and centralized feudal state after Qin Shihuang 秦始皇 unified China, though a degree of feudal separatism remained. . . . [1]

Thus the Qin dynasty was seen as marked simply by a change in the form of the state, and not by a transition from one mode of production to another. This is, of course, in flat contradiction with the views put forward in 1972-1974, in the context of the "Campaign to Criticize Lin Biao and Confucius." I shall come back to this point tomorrow in discussing Mao's last years.

In 1919, Mao Zedong had made what he called a "singular assertion": ". . . one day, the reform of the Chinese people will be more profound than that of any other people, and the society of the Chinese people will be more radiant than that of any other people."[2] Twenty years later, he once more expressed his faith in the exceptional capacities of his compatriots: "China has . . . given birth to many revolutionary strategists, statesmen, men of letters and thinkers. So the Chinese people [*minzu* 民族] is also a people with a glorious revolutionary tradition and a splendid historical heritage."[3]

Faithful to the sociological insights he had entertained in 1926, Mao gave particular credit to the peasants as participants in this revolutionary tradition. The "hundreds of peasant uprisings . . . and peasant wars" which had taken place over the centuries, on a "gigantic scale . . . without parallel in world history" were said to form the only "real motive force of China's historical evolution."

At the same time, Mao Zedong, whose thinking had become by the late 1930s much more explicitly Marxist in its framework of analysis, stressed the limitations on the capacity of such actions by the peasants alone, in a "feudal" society, to promote the development of the productive forces or change the mode of production, as opposed to simply serving as a tool for bringing about dynastic change. Without the "leadership of an advanced class and an advanced political party, such as the correct leadership given by the proletariat and the Communist Party today," these "peasant revolutions,"

[1] *Mao Zedong ji*, Vol. 7, pp. 100-101; *Selected Works*, II, pp. 307-308.
[2] *Mao Zedong ji*, Vol. 1, p. 69; translated in *The China Quarterly*, January-March 1972, p. 87.
[3] *Mao Zedong ji*, Vol. 7, p. 99; *Selected Works*, II, p. 306.

though they led to "some social progress," could only fail in the end.[4]

When and how, in Mao's view, did a situation arise in which the proletariat and the Communist Party could exercise "correct leadership" over the Chinese revolution? In the first stage, the "feudal" relations of production which had existed until the nineteenth century were partly broken down by the impact of the West, and the ensuing development of capitalism, and of an embryonic bourgeoisie. At this stage, although the landlords, backed by the imperialists, still dominated Chinese society, the bourgeois elements were the natural leaders of the revolutionary challenge to the existing order. Then, in a second stage, conditions became ripe for the proletariat to assert its hegemony over the revolution.

According to Mao Zedong, this transition took place roughly at the time of the May 4th Movement. The periods of bourgeois and proletarian hegemony he called respectively the "democratic" or "old democratic" and the "New Democratic" revolution. To the extent that Mao's theory of "New Democracy" dissociated the class character of a given historical stage from the class character of the actors in such a stage, by postulating that a "bourgeois-democratic" revolution could take place under the hegemony of the proletariat (or of its Party), he was simply following a view enunciated by Lenin (and in different terms by Trotsky) as early as 1905, and subsequently elaborated by Stalin as well. But although Mao's theory fitted into a tradition by then well established in the Communist movement, China around 1919 was far more backward economically, and the working class was far smaller there, than had been the case in Russia at the time of the 1905 revolution. How could Mao claim the leading role in the Chinese revolution for a class which, in the years 1915-1921, was only beginning to develop, and for a Party which counted, until the alliance with the Nationalists in 1923-1927, only a handful of members?

Apart from evoking the fact that the Communists enjoyed the support of the Soviet Union, Mao argued that the Chinese bourgeoisie and proletariat were "twins born of China's old . . . society, at once linked to each other and antagonistic to each other." Because the working class had emerged not only in Chinese-owned enterprises, but in those directly operated by the imperialists, " a very large section of the Chinese proletariat is older and more experienced than the Chinese bourgeoisie, and is therefore a greater and more broadly based social force."[5]

This is an ingenious argument, and not without substance. Primarily, however, Mao's assertion of proletarian hegemony from the May 4th period

---

[4]*Mao Zedong ji*, Vol. 7, p. 102; *Selected Works*, II, pp. 308-309.
[5]*Mao Zedong ji*, Vol. 7, pp. 104-105; *Selected Works*, II, p. 310.

onwards must be read not as a statement of fact, but as a claim that, from this moment, it was appropriate, and not wholly unrealistic, for the Communists to *strive* for leadership over the national revolution. And what was legitimate might not, at any given time, be expedient, or politically "correct." If the external threat from Japan to China's very existence as an independent state became so grave that the struggle against Japan replaced the struggle against Chiang Kaishek as the Communists' number one policy goal, and if the Guomindang was not only militarily stronger than the Communists, but willing to fight Japan, then it might be appropriate to accept, for a time, Guomindang leadership in such a struggle.

As I recalled last time, Mao had accepted by December 1935 the need for a new united front. He had agreed, in early 1937, following the Sian incident, that Chiang Kaishek must be the titular leader of such an alliance. In October 1938, in his report to the Sixth Plenum of the Central Committee (entitled "On the New Stage"), Mao went very far indeed in recognizing the leading role of the Guomindang, not only during the Anti-Japanese War, but in the phase of national reconstruction which would follow it. In a paragraph entitled "The Guomindang Has a Brilliant Future," he declared:

> ... The Guomindang and the Communist Party are the foundation of the Anti-Japanese United Front, but of these two it is the Guomindang that occupies first place. ... In the course of its glorious history, the Guomindang has been responsible for the overthrow of the Qing 清, the establishment of the Republic, ... and the great revolution of 1926-1927. Today it is once more leading the great Anti-Japanese War. ... It has had two great leaders in succession—Mr. Sun Yatsen and Mr. Chiang Kaishek. ...
>
> In carrying out the anti-Japanese war, and in organizing the Anti-Japanese United Front, the Guomindang occupies the position of leader and backbone [*jigan* 基幹] .... Under the single great condition that it support to the end the war of resistance and the United Front, one can foresee a brilliant future for the Guomindang. ...[6]

Nevertheless, this pronouncement was by no means the blank cheque which it might at first appear. The "single great condition" alone placed clear limits on the acceptance of Guomindang primacy, for if Chiang at any time failed to support and prosecute without reservations the war of resistance, his leadership could be repudiated. Indeed, to the extent that Mao regarded Chiang and the Guomindang as, in the long run, congenitally incapable of supporting unflinchingly the united front and the war against Japan, the time must come, in his view, when the Communists (whom Mao exhorted at the same time to "exercise the role of vanguard and model in every domain")

[6]*Mao Zedong ji*, Vol. 6, p. 198; translated in S. Schram, *The Political Thought of Mao Tse-tung*, pp. 228-229.

would have to pick up the fallen mantle. In fact, within a little more than a year, by the end of 1939, Mao's position had evolved to the point where he spoke of Communist leadership as already appropriate, and indeed as an accomplished fact.

Apart from considerations related to the international situation this more forceful attitude on Mao's part flowed from the immense strengthening of the political and military control of the Communists at the grass roots, which had expanded five-fold or more between 1938 and 1939.

Mao's line during the winter of 1939-1940 varied depending on the audience he was addressing, but not fundamentally. In *On New Democracy*, aimed at "third force" intellectuals, the bald claim to Communist leadership was covered with a rhetorical fig leaf. If the Chinese bourgeoisie should prove itself capable of leading the people in "driving out Japanese imperialism and introducing democratic government . . . , no one will be able to refuse his admiration [*shui bu neng bu peifu ta* 誰不能不佩服他]." Otherwise, this responsibility would "inevitably fall on the shoulders of the proletariat."[7] Plainly, that is what Mao expected to happen, and in *The Chinese Revolution and the Chinese Communist Party*, written mainly for an audience of Party members (though it was on open sale), he said so quite unambiguously. And in his Introduction to the inner-Party periodical *The Communist*, written in October 1939, Mao did not even raise the question of who should exercise hegemony; he simply assumed that leadership belonged to the communists, and proceeded to discuss how they should go about exercising it.[8]

As for the forces supporting the revolution at the time of the Anti-Japanese War, Mao's view was reasonably consistent, whatever the audience he was writing for. He saw them as composed of Stalin's four-class bloc of the 1920s, with the addition of a certain portion of the "comprador bourgeoisie" tied to powers whose interests were in conflict with those of Japan. The original version of *On New Democracy* does, however, exhibit one curious anomaly: it refers throughout to a three-class, rather than a four-class bloc. The difference is of form rather than of substance, but is not without interest. It results from lumping together the peasantry (which has always been regarded by Marxists as petty bourgeois in nature) with the urban petty bourgeoisie, and calling the resulting category *"the"* petty bourgeoisie, instead of counting the peasants as a separate class.[9]

[7]*Mao Zedong ji*, Vol. 7, p. 162; translated in Carrere d'Encausse and Schram, *Marxism and Asia*, p. 254.

[8]*Mao Zedong ji*, Vol. 7, pp. 80-81, 129; translated in *Selected Works*, II, pp. 294-295, and S. Schram, *The Political Thought of Mao Tse-tung*, pp. 230-231.

[9]*Mao Zedong ji*, Vol. 7, p. 196; translated in Carrere d'Encausse and Schram, *Marxism and Asia*, pp. 256-257.

It is quite clear that the swallowing-up of the peasantry in the catch-all category of the "petty bourgeoisie" served to attenuate the emphasis on the unique character of China's revolution, and especially on one of its original traits: guerrilla warfare in the countryside. In his Introduction to *The Communist*, Mao stressed, on the contrary, the uniqueness of China's experience, and in particular the importance of armed struggle. "Comrade Stalin," he recalled, "has said, 'In China the armed people are fighting armed counter-revolution. That is one of the specific features of the Chinese revolution.' This is perfectly true."[10] The quotation from Stalin is a particularly cynical instance of citing out of context: when Stalin made this statement in December 1926 the "armed people" he was talking about were represented by Chiang Kaishek, in whose fidelity to the cause he still had full confidence, and Mao knew this very well. Still, the point was well taken.

In this same text of October 1939, Mao characterized the united front, armed struggle, and Party building as the Chinese Communist Party's "three magic weapons." The place of armed struggle in Mao's strategy requires no further comment here. As for the united front, his essential message was that it should be marked by both unity and struggle. Its form was to be the "joint dictatorship of all the revolutionary classes."[11]

Finally, the third of Mao's "magic weapons," Party building, meant not simply developing the Party organization, but defining a correct doctrine, and unifying and rectifying the Party on the basis of that doctrine. That was precisely the goal of the "Sinification of Marxism" for which Mao called in October 1938, and which he sought to carry out between 1938 and 1943.

This slogan was in fact used by the Chinese communists only for a relatively short period, which began in 1938, when Mao first made the term his own, and reached its culmination in 1945 when, at the Seventh Party Congress, Liu Shaoqi 劉少奇 hailed Mao's gigantic achievements in creating theories which were "thoroughly Marxist, and at the same time thoroughly Chinese." But if the term itself was relatively ephemeral, the concerns it expresses were present before 1938, and not only survived but grew in importance after the establishment of the Chinese People's Republic, and especially from the early 1960s.

To call for the "nationalization" of Marxism (as Liu Shaoqi put it in 1945) implies the adaptation of Marxist theories to national reality at many different levels, from language and culture to the economic and social structure of largely pre-capitalist agrarian societies. Moreover, the question also arises as to which "Marxism," or what elements of Marxism, are to be Sinified. The

[10]*Mao Zedong ji*, Vol. 7, p. 72; *Selected Works*, II, pp. 286-287.
[11]This formulation is from "On New Democracy," *Mao Zedong ji*, Vol. 7, p. 154; translated in Carrère d'Encausse and Schram, *Marxism and Asia*, p. 252.

intermingling of the various dimensions of the phenomenon is evoked in Mao Zedong's classic statement regarding Sinification, in October 1938, when he said in part:

> Today's China is an outgrowth of historic China. We are Marxist historicists; we must not mutilate history. From Confucius to Sun Yat-sen we must sum it up critically, and we must constitute ourselves the heirs to this precious legacy. Conversely, the assimilation of this legacy itself becomes a method that aids considerably in guiding the present great movement. A communist is a Marxist internationalist, but Marxism must take on a national form before it can be of any practical effect. There is no such thing as abstract Marxism, but only concrete Marxism. What we call concrete Marxism is Marxism that has taken on a national form, that is, Marxism applied to the concrete struggle in the concrete conditions prevailing in China, and not Marxism abstractly used. Consequently, the Sinification of Marxism—that is to say, making certain that in all of its manifestations it is imbued with Chinese characteristics, using it according to Chinese peculiarities —becomes a problem that must be understood and solved by the whole Party without delay. We must put an end to writing eight-legged essays on foreign models; we must discard our dogmatism and replace it by a new and vital Chinese style and manner, pleasing to the eye and to the ear of the Chinese common people. . . .[12]

Obviously, if Marxism is to have any impact in a non-European country, it must be presented to the people of that country in language which is vivid and meaningful in the light of their mentality and traditions. But such Sinification of the form of Marxism, though indispensable in Mao's view, was only the outward manifestation of a more fundamental enterprise, aiming to transform the very substance of Marxism in order to adapt it to Chinese conditions.

Consider Mao Zedong's statement: "There is no such thing as abstract Marxism, but only concrete Marxism." In the light of Mao's words and actions both in Yan'an and in later years, the ideas underlying this assertion could be spelled out roughly as follows. The theory of scientific socialism was first expounded by Marx. Certain aspects of his writings are of universal validity, but the theory as a whole reflects both its origins in the nineteenth century, and Marx's specifically European mentality and experience. When we talk, therefore (like Stalin and everyone else from Lenin on down), about applying the universally valid principles of Marxism to Chinese conditions, it is the timeless kernel of these theories which we should seek to grasp and adapt to our needs.

And what is that timeless kernel? Mao himself declared, in October 1938: "We must not study the letter of Marxism-Leninism, but the standpoint and

[12] *Mao Zedong ji*, Vol. 6, pp. 260-261; translated in S. Schram, *The Political Thought of Mao Tse-tung*, pp. 172-173.

method of its creators, with which they observed and solved problems."
In February 1942, he called upon his comrades of the Chinese Communist
Party to "take the standpoint, viewpoint and methods of Marxism-Leninism,"
and apply them to China.[13]

These formulations raise two problems: What did Mao mean by "standpoint," "viewpoint," and "methods"? And what was the relation between such
attitudes or principles derived from Marxism, and the "method" which, he said,
could be derived from the assimilation of the precious legacy of China's past?

As for the first point, the current Chinese interpretation is that Mao was
talking about adopting the standpoint of the proletariat, the viewpoint of
historical materialism, and the method of dialectics. But if Mao was indeed
referring to aspects of Marxism as broadly defined as these, does it not follow
that, in his view, the theories of Marx himself constituted in fact "German
Marxism," just as the ideas of Lenin were characterized by his critics in the
early twentieth century as "Russian Marxism"? In other words, by "abstract
Marxism," Mao perhaps meant "absolute Marxism," or Marxist theory uncon-
ditionally valid in all countries and at all times. And when he said that such
Marxism "did not exist," he seemed to be suggesting that Marx's own writings
did not have the status of a higher-level general theory, but were merely one
concrete incarnation of the standpoint, viewpoint, and methods which he had
devised, in no way superior to the application of the same principles by
Stalin, or by Mao himself.

For Mao it was not, however, merely a question of applying Marxism to
China; he also proposed as we have seen to enrich it with elements drawn
from China's experience. Nor were the "Chinese peculiarities" with which
Mao proposed to imbue his Marxism merely the economic traits China shared
with other Asian countries. They were also the "precious qualities" which, as
he put it in 1938, had been exhibited "in the history of our great people over
several millennia," and had been shaped both by historical experience and by
the genius of the Chinese people.

Precisely how central this theme was to Mao's whole vision of revolution
in China is indicated by the extraordinary statement, in the passage quoted
earlier, that the assimilation of the Chinese heritage "itself becomes a method
that aids considerably in guiding the present great movement."

The suggestion that a deeper knowledge of the past will not merely widen
the revolutionaries' understanding of their own society, but will actually
provide an instrument for leading the revolution, opens vistas without
precedent in the history of Marxism down to 1938.

[13] *Mao Zedong ji*, Vol. 8, p. 75; translated in S. Schram, *The Political Thought of
Mao Tse-tung*, pp. 179-180.

What was the nature of this method, which Mao said could be distilled from the experience of "historic China," and which elements in the past were to be drawn upon in producing it? He did not spell this out explicitly, but there are hints that he was thinking about a domain which could be loosely defined as that of the art of statecraft. Thus, in another section of the report of October 1938 in which he first put forward the idea of Sinification, Mao dealt with the problem of making proper use of cadres—which, he said, had been referred to in the past as "employing people in the administration" [yongren xingzheng 用人行政]. He went on to discuss the continuity between the present and the past in the following terms:

> Throughout our national history there have been two sharply contrasting lines on the subject of the use of cadres, reflecting the opposition between the depraved and the upright, one being to "appoint people on their merit," and the other being "to appoint people by favouritism." The former was the policy of sagacious rulers and worthy ministers in making appointments; the latter was that of despots and traitors. Today, when we talk about making use of cadres, it is from a revolutionary standpoint, fundamentally different from that of ancient times, and yet there is no getting away from this standard of "appointing people on their merit."[14]

The next main phase in the development of Mao Zedong's ideas, in 1941-1943, was much more directly linked to conflicts with his rivals in the Party, and the views he propagated were explicitly designed to serve his interests in that struggle.

These lectures are concerned rather with ideas than with historical fact. The following succinct chronology brings out clearly, however, the concrete significance of certain theoretical statements:

5 May, 1941   Mao makes a speech to a cadre meeting in Yan'an criticizing "scholars of Marxism-Leninism" who "can only repeat quotes from Marx, Engels, Lenin, and Stalin from memory, but about their own ancestors . . . have to apologize and say they've forgotten."

1 July, 1941   Adoption of Central Committee resolution on "strengthening the Party spirit," stressing the importance of discipline and of absolute subordination of cadres at all levels to higher authority.

13 July, 1941   Sun Yefang 孫冶方 writes a letter to Liu Shaoqi (using the pen name Song Liang 宋亮), referring to the two opposing deviations of slighting theoretical study and scholasticism, and asking for some "Chinese examples" of the correct

[14] *Mao Zedong ji*, Vol. 6, pp. 250-251.

	relation between theory and practice. Liu replies the same day stressing the difficulties of Sinifying Marxism, and blaming the lack of progress thus far partly on the fact that few Chinese Communist Party members can read Marx in the original.
23 Jan., 1942	Mao orders army cadres to study his Gutian Resolution of December 1929 until they are thoroughly familiar with it.
1 Feb. and 8 Feb., 1942	Mao delivers his two keynote speeches on Rectification. In the second of these, he complains that his 1938 call for "Sinification" has not been heeded.
May 1942	Mao delivers two talks to the Yan'an Forum on Literature and Art, but these are not published for nearly a year and a half.
Dec. 1942	Mao delivers a report *On Economic and Financial Problems*.
March 1943	Central Committee elects Mao Chairman of the Central Committee and Chairman of the Politburo of the Chinese Communist Party.
26 May, 1943	Mao, commenting on the dissolution of the Comintern, declares that, although Moscow has not meddled in the affairs of the Chinese Communist Party since the Seventh Comintern Congress of August 1935, the Chinese Communists have done their work very well.
1 June, 1943	Resolution, drafted by Mao, on methods of leadership puts forward the classic formulation of the "mass line."
6 July, 1943	Liu Shaoqi publishes the article "Liquidate Menshevik Thought in the Party," hailing Mao as a true Bolshevik and denouncing the "international faction" as Mensheviks in disguise.
July 1943	Movement to investigate cadres started in Yan'an—in fact, a harsh purge of anti-Maoist elements in the Party, under the control of Kang Sheng 康生.
19 Oct., 1943	Mao's "Yan'an Talks" finally published in *Jiefang ribao* 解放日報.
April 1945	Mao's thought written into the Party Constitution as the guide to all the Party's work, and Mao hailed by Liu Shaoqi for his earth-shaking contributions in "Sinifying" or "nationalizing" Marxism.[15]

[15] Most of these events are well known, and since my main concern in these lectures is with ideas rather than with facts, I shall not footnote them all in detail. Liu Shaoqi's article of 6 July, 1943, originally published in *Jiefang ribao*, is translated in Boyd Compton, *Mao's China. Party Reform Documents, 1942-1944* (Seattle: University of Washington Press, 1952). His letter to Song Liang (now identified as Sun Yefang) has

If we accept that Mao, after his humiliation at the hands of the "28 Bol-sheviks" in 1932-1934, and a long hard struggle, from 1935 to 1943, to establish his own political and ideological authority, at length achieved this goal in the course of the Rectification Campaign, what sort of political and economic system did he establish at that time in the Yan'an base area, and what were the principles underlying it? It has been repeatedly argued that the essence of the Yan'an heritage lies in an intimate relationship between the Party and the masses. There is much truth in this, but the matter should not be looked at too one-sidedly.

To work with the people did not mean for Mao to lose oneself in them, in some great orgy of populist spontaneity. Nor should the Yan'an heritage be romanticized, or sentimentalized, to make Mao a believer in some kind of "extended democracy" with overtones of anarchism. The classic directive of 1 June, 1943 itself, in which Mao first formulated systematically his ideas on the mass line, makes this plain enough, if properly understood. The key passage, with which you are certainly all familiar, reads:

> ... all correct leadership is necessarily from the masses, to the masses. This means: take the ideas of the masses (scattered and unsystematic ideas) and concentrate them (through study turn them into concentrated and systematic ideas), then go to the masses and propagate and explain these ideas *until the masses embrace them as their own* [*hua wei qunzhong de yijian* 化爲群衆的意見], hold fast to them and translate them into action, and test the correctness of these ideas in such action. ...[16]

In other words, the people were to be made to interiorize ideas which they were quite incapable of elaborating for themselves. There is a remarkable parallel between this last phrase and Lenin's view that class consciousness could only be imported into the proletariat from outside. It is therefore not surprising that a year earlier, in his speech of 1 February, 1942 launching the Rectification Campaign, Mao should have reaffirmed in its full Leninist rigour the "system of democratic centralism, in which the minority is subject to the majority, the lower level to the higher level, the part to the whole, and the entire membership to the Central Committee."

At the same time, it must be recognized that Mao's view according to which ordinary people may be a source of ideas from which correct policies are elaborated, and that they can in turn understand these policies, rather than blindly applying them, marked a very great rupture with one of the central themes of traditional Chinese thought. According to the *Analects*: "The people may be made to follow a path of action, but they may not be

---

recently been officially published in *Hongqi* 紅旗, no. 7, 1980, pp. 2-4. Liu's report of April 1945 has recently been reprinted in China, both in English and in Chinese.

[16] *Selected Works*, III, pp. 117-122.

made to understand it."[17] Mao argued that they could be *made* to understand
it, but he was no more prepared than Lenin to assume that the people would
spontaneously do the right thing, or to abdicate the responsibilities of leadership.

Within the broad limits defined by Mao's insistence both on a measure of
initiative and involvement from below, and on firm centralized guidance from
above, there is room for an infinite variety of shades of emphasis. From
Yan'an days onwards, Mao Zedong rang the changes on these themes. Consistently, however, at least until the Cultural Revolution, he regarded centralized
leadership as in the last analysis even more important than democracy.

In Yan'an days, a key slogan in economic work was "centralized leadership
and dispersed operation" [*jizhong lingdao, fensan jingying* 集中領導，分散
經營]. Such an approach was particularly appropriate in circumstances where
only a relatively small proportion of the total area controlled by the Communists was located in the main Yan'an base area, and the technical level of the
economy was so low that centralized planning of inputs and outputs was
neither possible nor desirable. Even under these circumstances, however, the
accent was by no means on continued dispersion of responsibility and effort.
In his report of December 1942 *On Economic and Financial Problems*, Mao
explained that it was necessary to decentralize production to some extent, in
order to promote "enthusiam" at the lower levels, but that "unlimited
dispersal" was not profitable, and that the overall pattern of management must
therefore undergo a "process of dispersal at first and centralization later."[18]

Centralized leadership, in Mao's view, could of course come only from the
Party. A key concept, introduced at about this time, which conveys the
essence of the Party's unifying and guiding role was "*yiyuanhua*" 一元化—
literally, "to make one," "to make monolithic," and perhaps most appro-
priately translated into English as "to integrate." The meaning of this term is
clearly defined and illustrated in the decision of 1 June, 1943, in which Mao
declares:

> In relaying to subordinate units any task . . . , a higher organization should in all
> cases go through the leader of the lower organization concerned, so that he may
> assume responsibility, thus achieving the goal of combining division of labour
> with integrated [*yiyuanhua*] leadership. A department at higher level should not
> go solely to its counterpart at the lower level (for instance, a higher department
> concerned with organization, propaganda or counter-espionage should not go
> solely to the corresponding department at the lower level), leaving the person in

---

[17]*Analects*, Book VIII, Ch. ix, in Legge, *The Chinese Classics*, Vol. I, p. 211.

[18]*Mao Zedong ji*, Vol. 8, pp. 263-264; Andrew Watson, *Mao Zedong and the Political
Economy of the Border Region* (Cambridge: Cambridge University Press, 1980),
pp. 149-150. (Only the first part of this very long report appears in the *Selected Works*.)

overall charge of the lower organization (such as the secretary, the chairman, the director or the school principal) in ignorance or without responsibility.[19]

The sense, plainly, is that the necessary division of labour between various organs can exist without posing a threat to the unity of the movement only on condition that the whole system be penetrated and controlled by a unifying force in the shape of the Party. In other words, *yiyuanhua* or integration naturally goes together with the principle of "dual rule," implemented in Yan'an and resuscitated in 1956, under which no administrative or economic unit can run its own affairs without constant and active intervention by the Party.

When the prospect of a "coalition government" with the Guomindang, which Mao had envisaged as a useful tactical expedient in 1944-1945, finally evaporated in 1946, and was replaced by open civil war, there was no longer any reason for maintaining the slightest ambiguity about the Party's immediate political goals. Mao therefore spelled out, on 30 June, 1949, in an article written to commemorate the twenty-eighth anniversary of the foundation of the Chinese Communist Party, the precise nature of the "People's Democratic Dictatorship" which he proposed to establish three months later.

As for the class nature of the new state, Mao defined the locus of authority in terms of what has often been called a concentric-circle metaphor. The "people" who were to exercise the dictatorship would be composed of the working class, the peasantry, the urban petty bourgeoisie, and the "national bourgeoisie." Of these four classes, the workers would enjoy hegemony, and the peasants constituted their most reliable allies. The petty bourgeoisie were to be largely followers, while the national bourgeoisie had a dual nature: they were part of the people, but at the same time exploiters. Consequently, those elements among them who behaved badly could be re-classified as "non-people," and find themselves on the receiving end of the dictatorship, the objects rather than the subjects of revolutionary change.

Mao made no mystery at all of the form of the state which was to represent these four classes. Replying to imaginary critics who complained that the communists were "autocrats," he declared:

> My dear sirs, you are right, that is just what we are. All the experience the Chinese people have accumulated through several decades teaches us to enforce the people's democratic dictatorship—which one could also call people's democratic autocracy, the two terms mean the same thing—that is, to deprive the reactionaries of the right to speak and let the people alone have that right. . . .
> Don't you want to abolish state power? Yes, we do, but not right now; we cannot do it yet. Why? Because imperialism still exists, because domestic reaction still exists, because classes still exist in our country. Our present task is to

[19]*Mao Zedong ji*, Vol. 9, p. 29; *Selected Works*, III, pp. 120-121.

strengthen the people's state apparatus—mainly the people's army, the people's police, and the people's courts—in order to consolidate the national defence and protect the people's interests. Given this condition, China can develop steadily, under the leadership of the working class and the Communist Party, from an agricultural into an industrial country, and from a new-democratic into a socialist and communist society, abolish classes and realize the Great Harmony [*datong* 大同].

In this task of guiding the development of China "from an agricultural into an industrial country," Mao said that "the education of the peasantry" was "the serious problem." For, he added: "The peasant economy is scattered, and the socialization of agriculture, judging by the Soviet Union's experience, will require a long time and painstaking work."[20]

These brief quotations evoke several crucial dimensions of the problem of the implementation of Marxist revolution in China after 1949. On the one hand, Mao's theory of the "People's Democratic Dictatorship" was the lineal descendent of Lenin's "Revolutionary-Democratic Dictatorship of the Workers and Peasants," and of Stalin's "Four-Class Bloc," and Mao himself freely acknowledged this ideological debt, and went out of his way to stress the relevance of Soviet experience. Indeed, however unorthodox his road to power, as soon as victory was plainly within his grasp, Mao had announced his intention of doing things henceforth in the orthodox way. "From 1927 to the present," he declared in March 1949, "the centre of gravity of our work has been in the villages—gathering strength in the villages in order to surround the cities, and then taking the cities. The period for this method of work has now ended. The period of 'from the city to the village' and of the city leading the village has now begun. The centre of gravity of the Party's work has shifted from the village to the city."

Hence the stress on educating the peasants, and on working-class leadership of the "people's dictatorship," which was to do the educating. Hence the attempt, which was to be made in the early 1950s, to draw large numbers of real flesh-and-blood workers into the Chinese Communist Party, in order to "improve" its class composition.

And yet, despite all this, and despite Mao's explicit statement, in 1962, that during these early years there had been no alternative to "copying from the Soviets," his article of 30 June, 1949 itself contained elements pointing in a significantly different direction. Thus the old-fashioned word "*ducai*" 獨裁 or autocracy was used as a synonym for dictatorship (*zhuanzheng* 專政). Too much should not be made of this point, for this compound had sometimes been employed in years past, when Marxist expressions did not all have standard equivalents in Chinese, as a translation for "dictatorship." Mao

[20]*Selected Works*, IV, pp. 418-419.

cannot, however, have been unaware of the traditional overtones *ducai* would have for his readers, any more than he was unaware of the connotations of the term *datong*, which he used as an equivalent for communism.

In 1953, when a committee headed by Mao was engaged in drafting a Constitution for the People's Republic of China, an eight-line rhyme was coined to sum up the criteria for the proper functioning of the political system:

> Great power is monopolized,
> Small power is dispersed.
> The Party committee takes decisions,
> All quarters carry them out.
> Implementation also involves decisions,
> But they must not depart from principles.
> Checking on the work
> Is the responsibility of the Party committee.[21]

Expounding the meaning of this poem in January 1958 (in the context of the Great Leap Forward, to which I shall turn in a moment), Mao declared:

"Great power is monopolized" [*daquan dulan* 大權獨攬] is a cliché which is customarily used to refer to the arbitrary decisions of an individual [*geren duduan* 個人獨斷]. We borrow this phrase to indicate that the main powers should be concentrated in collective bodies such as the Central Committee and local Party committees, we use it to oppose dispersionism. Can it possibly be argued that great power should be scattered?[22]

The general thrust is plain enough, and corresponds entirely to other statements by Mao during the late 1950s and early 1960s. Thus, in his speech of 25 April, 1956, "On the Ten Great Relationships," Mao argued in favour of a "further extension of local power," which he found "too limited," and hence not conducive to the enthusiasm at the gross roots required in order to build socialism effectively. But at the same time, he added:

Naturally we must at the same time tell comrades at the lower levels that they should not act wildly. . . . Where they can conform, they ought to conform. . . . Where they cannot conform . . . , then conformity should not be sought at all costs. In short, the localities should have an appropriate degree of power. This would be beneficial to the building of a strong socialist state.[23]

In his speech of January 1962, after asserting that centralism and democracy must be combined "both within the Party and outside," and stressing once again, as he had in Yan'an, that centralism was even more important than

---

[21] "Sixty Articles on Work Methods," *Current Background*, no. 892, p. 9; Chinese in *Wan-sui* 萬歲 (Supplement), p. 34.

[22] *Wan-sui* (Supplement), pp. 34-35; my translation.

[23] S. Schram (ed.), *Mao Tse-tung Unrehearsed* (Harmondsworth: Penguin, 1974), p. 73.

democracy, Mao went on to say that genuine centralization was possible only on a basis of democracy, for two main reasons. On the one hand, if people were not allowed to express themselves, they would be "angry" and frustrated, and therefore would not participate willingly and effectively in political and economic work. And on the other hand:

> If there is no democracy, if ideas are not coming from the masses, it is impossible to establish a good line. . . . Our leading organs merely play the role of a processing plant in the establishment of a good line and good . . . policies and methods. Everyone knows that if a factory has no raw material, it cannot do any processing. . . . Without democracy, you have no understanding of what is happening down below; the general situation will be unclear; . . . and thus you will find it difficult to avoid being subjectivist; it will be impossible to achieve unity of understanding and unity of action, and impossible to achieve true centralism.[24]

Here the term "democratic centralism" is made to cover both the fundamental dilemma of combining effective "centralized unification" with active support and initiative from below, and the problem of the upward and downward flow of ideas evoked by the slogan of the "mass line." Mao's overall view of this cluster of issues is clearly reflected in the metaphor of the "processing plant." To be sure, this plant is incapable of producing anything meaningful if it is not constantly fed with information and suggestions, but in the last analysis the correct line can only be elaborated by the brain at the centre. The deprecatory adverb "merely" before "processing plant" does not change the fact that this is where the decisive action takes place.

Such was Mao's line on democracy and centralism, from Yan'an days to the early 1960s. It is widely thought that he departed from this overriding emphasis on centralized authority at the time of the Cultural Revolution. That problem I shall take up tomorrow. Meanwhile, let us look at other aspects of Mao's thought before, during and after the Great Leap Forward.

In approaching Mao's ideas regarding patterns of socialist development, it is perhaps worth emphasizing by way of introduction that his attitude toward modernization and industrialization was consistently positive. There has been a tendency in recent years to treat Mao as a believer in some kind of pastoral utopia, a partisan of a "steady-state" economy as an alternative to our so-called advanced industrial society. In reality, throughout the twenty-seven years during which he presided over the destinies of the People's Republic of China, Mao never ceased to call for rapid economic progress, and for progress defined in quantitative terms: tons of steel, tons of grain, and all the rest.

The very use of the term "modernization" was often taken, in the recent past, as a manifestation of Western cultural arrogance, because it seemed to imply that in joining the "modern" world, the peoples of Asia and Africa

[24]*Ibid.*, pp. 163-164.

would necessarily become like the Americans or the Europeans. This does not in fact follow; no one can deny that Japan has achieved a high degree of modernization, and yet that country has not become Westernized except in relatively superficial respects. In any case, apart from the fact that the Chinese government has recently turned modernization into one of its key slogans, Mao Zedong himself repeatedly characterized China's economic aims in these terms.

There can be no doubt that scientific and technical modernization was a central and crucial strand in Mao's conception of socialist development. Unlike the Soviets, Mao did not confuse the industrial revolution with the socialist revolution, but he did regard it as an indispensable precondition for establishing a socialist society. But were his broader goals compatible with such technical modernization?

I do not accept the view, commonly put forward a decade ago, according to which the economic model advocated by Mao in the late 1950s constituted simply "the revival of the Yan'an heritage." While it is true that there are significant hints of what was to come in the experience of the Yan'an base areas, these beginnings were too one-sided to justify the conclusion that the ideas of the Great Leap were implicit in them. They involved only a stress on indigenous methods, and not large-scale inputs or modern technology, which did not exist in Yan'an. The only true element of continuity from the 1940s to the 1950s to the 1960s was the theme of self-reliance.

If we look at Mao's economic ideas during and after the Great Leap as formulated at the time, we must recognize, in my opinion, that they are far less one-sided and simplistic than they have commonly been made out to be in recent years, in interpretations based on the Cultural Revolution reconstruction of the "struggle between two lines." We find him placing stress equally on moral *and* material incentives, on redness *and* expertise, and on large and small-scale industry. The policy of "walking on two legs," which was in some respects the heart of his whole economic strategy, was a policy of walking as fast as possible on both of these legs, and not of hopping along on the leg of small-scale indigenous methods alone.

And yet, there are aspects of Mao Zedong's approach to development even during the period of the Great Leap, which reflect a fundamental ambiguity toward the implications of industrialization and technical progress. Two crucial points are the role of the intellectuals, and the role of the peasantry, in the revolution.

In 1949, Mao had declared, as I noted earlier, "The serious problem is the education of the peasantry." The implication plainly was that these rural dwellers would have to be brought into the modern world by causing them to assimilate knowledge, and especially technical knowledge, originating in the

cities. And in this process, scientists, technicians, and other intellectuals would have a key role to play. Indeed, Mao recognized this in January 1956 when he declared, in the context of his Twelve-Year Programme for Agricultural Development, that the Chinese people "must have a far-reaching comprehensive plan of work in accordance with which they could strive to wipe out China's economic, scientific, and cultural backwardness within a few decades and rapidly get abreast of the most advanced nations in the world." And he added that "to achieve this great goal, the decisive factor was to have cadres, to have an adequate number of excellent scientists and technicians."[25]

Mao therefore called, in January 1956, for a conciliatory and understanding approach to the intellectuals inherited from the old society, and launched in May 1956 the "Hundred Flowers" campaign, designed to rally their active support for building socialism. What happened during the ensuing year is well known to all of you. The result was that Mao, angered (and discredited in the eyes of his colleagues) by the harsh and to his mind negative and destructive criticisms of the intellectuals turned savagely against them. Henceforth, apart from training new, red intellectuals of good class origin (which he called, suggestively, "our own *xiucai* 秀才 "), Mao Zedong would rely rather on the enthusiasm and creativity of the masses.

As for these wretched bookworms who had failed to respond to his call in 1956-1957, who needed them? Mao therefore made repeated statements, and actively promoted policies, entirely at variance with his view of 1956 that scientists were the decisive factor, stressing that "all wisdom comes from the masses," and that "the intellectuals are most ignorant." In March 1958, he declared:

> Ever since ancient times the people who founded new schools of thought were all young people without much learning. They had the ability to recognize new things at a glance and, having grasped them, opened fire on the old fogeys. . . . Franklin of America, who discovered electricity, began as a newspaper boy. . . . Gorki only had two years of elementary schooling. Of course, some things can be learned at school; I don't propose to close all the schools. What I mean is that it is not absolutely necessary to attend school.[26]

At the same time, Mao repudiated the fetishism of technology which characterized, in his view, the Soviet approach to economic development, In his comments of 1958 or 1959 on Stalin's *Economic Problems of Socialism in the USSR*, Mao noted ". . . [the Soviets] are concerned only with the relations of production, they do not pay attention to the super-structure, they do not pay attention to politics, they do not pay attention to the role of

[25] Speech of 25 January, 1956, in H. Carrère d'Encausse and S. Schram, *Marxism and Asia*, p. 293; *Renmin ribao* 人民日報 , 26 January, 1956.
[26] S. Schram, *Mao Tse-tung Unrehearsed*, pp. 119-120.

the people. Without a communist movement, it is impossible to reach communism."[27]

From the mid-1950s onwards, the "communist movement" Mao envisaged consisted above all in mobilizing in the countryside the peasants, who for their part had not disappointed him during the co-operativization drive of 1955-56. In December 1955, he wrote:

> If you compare our country with the Soviet Union: (1) we had twenty years' experience in the base areas, and were trained in three revolutionary wars; our experience [on coming to power] was exceedingly rich. . . . Therefore, we are able to set up a state very quickly, and complete the tasks of the revolution. (The Soviet Union was a newly-established state; at the time of the October Revolution, they had neither army nor government apparatus, and there were very few Party members. (2) We enjoy the assistance of the Soviet Union and other democratic countries. (3) Our population is very numerous, and our position is excellent. [Our people] work industriously and bear much hardship, and there is no way out for the peasants without co-operativization. Chinese peasants are even better than English and American workers. Consequently, we can reach socialism more, better and faster. . . .[28]

Thus, Mao suggested as early as 1955 that because they came to power after twenty years' struggle in the countryside, instead of by suddenly seizing the reins of government in the capital city, the Chinese communists knew more in 1949 than Lenin and his comrades had known in 1917 about exercising authority over the population at the grass roots and securing their support. Moreover, the Chinese peasantry, in his view, provided remarkable human material for building a socialist society, and the peasants had to be given their full role in the process.

To give them their full role did not, however, mean for Mao to place them on the same level as the workers. "The peasants," he said at the first Zhengzhou Conference of November 1958, in the aftermath of the Great Leap Forward, "after all remain peasants, throughout the whole period when the system of ownership by the whole people has not yet been implemented in the countryside, they after all retain a certain dual nature on the road to socialism." At the Second Zhengzhou Conference of February-March 1959, he reiterated this statement several times, adding that at the present stage the workers, not the peasants, still played the role of "elder brother" in the relationship between the two.[29]

Perhaps Mao never truly resolved, either in practice or in his own mind,

[27] *Wan-sui* (1967), pp. 156-157.
[28] *Wan-sui* (1969), p. 27; translated in S. Schram, "The Marxist," in D. Wilson (ed.), *Mao Tse-tung in the Scales of History* (Cambridge: Cambridge University Press, 1977), p. 51.
[29] *Wan-sui* (1969), p. 247; *Wan-sui* (1967), pp. 12, 17, 49 etc.

the dilemma of a peasantry which was simultaneously the salt of the earth, and the "younger brother" of the working class in building socialism. In any case, the ambiguity of his views is reflected in the fact that the "people's communes," set up in the countryside in the summer of 1958, were hailed as the building-blocks of a future communist society. Moreover, it was explicitly stated, in a resolution of December 1958, that the cities lagged behind the countryside in this domain because "bourgeois consciousness" was still rife in the urban environment.

There is an echo here of the thesis, repeatedly expounded by Mao between 1956 and 1958, according to which the Chinese people could draw positive advantages from the fact that they were "poor and blank." "Poor people," he wrote in April 1958, "want change, want to do things, want revolution. A clean sheet of paper has no blotches, and so the newest and most beautiful words can be written on it, the newest and most beautiful pictures can be painted on it."[30] To the extent that the peasants were even blanker than the Chinese people as a whole, that is, even more innocent of the wiles of the modern world, they were evidently superior in virtue, and in revolutionary capacities.

Perhaps the most striking and suggestive symbol of the overall pattern of socialist development which Mao Zedong sought to promote at the time of the Great Leap Forward was the theory of the "permanent" or "uninterrupted" revolution, which he defined as follows in the "Sixty Articles on Work Methods" of January 1958:

> Our revolutions follow each other, one after another. Beginning with the seizure of power on a nation-wide scale in 1949, there followed first the anti-feudal land reform; as soon as land reform was completed, agricultural co-operativization was begun. . . . The three great socialist transformations, that is to say the socialist revolution in the ownership of the means of production, were basically completed in 1956. Following this, we carried out last year the socialist revolution on the political and ideological fronts [i.e., the anti-rightist campaign]. . . . But the problem is still not resolved, and for a fairly long period to come, the method of airing of views and rectification must be used every year to solve the problems in this field. We must now have a technical revolution, in order to catch up with and overtake England in fifteen years or a bit longer. . . .[31]

As this passage makes plain, it was characteristic of the Great Leap Forward, as of Mao's approach to revolution generally, that economic, social, political, and cultural transformation was to be carried out simultaneously. At the same time, as I have already stressed, a dramatic raising both of technical

[30] *Hongqi*, 1 June, 1958, pp. 3-4; *Peking Review*, no. 15, 10 June, 1958, p. 6.
[31] *Wan-sui* (Supplement), pp. 32-33; translation from S. Schram, "Mao Tse-tung and the Theory of the Permanent Revolution," *The China Quarterly*, April-June 1971, pp. 226-227.

levels, and of levels of material production, was very much part of the Maoist vision in 1958.

Twice, indeed, in the course of the radical phase of the Great Leap, Mao dated the beginnings of the process of modernization and change in China from the moment when, at the end of the nineteenth century, Zhang Zhidong 張之 洞 embarked on his programme of industrialization. In September 1958, he measured progress in terms of numbers of machine tools; in February 1959, his criterion was the growth of the Chinese working class. In both cases, he compared China's achievements before and after 1949 in catching up with the more advanced countries of the world.[32]

This does not mean, of course, that Mao regarded industrialization, or even economic development in general, as the whole essence of revolution. In a speech at the Second Session of the Eighth Party Congress in May 1958, at which the Great Leap Forward was officially proclaimed, he asserted his resolve to press ahead with rapid economic growth, but indicated that revolution would not result from development alone:

> We do not put forward the slogans "Cadres decide everything" and "Technology decides everything," nor do we put forward the slogan "Communism equals the Soviets plus electrification." Since we do not put forward this slogan, does this mean that we won't electrify? We will electrify just the same, and even a bit more fiercely. The first two slogans were formulated by Stalin, they are one-sided. [If you say] "Technology decides everything"—what about politics? [If you say] "Cadres decide everything"—what about the masses? This is not sufficiently dialectical.[33]

Thus, although China intended to "electrify," i.e. to develop her economy (in Lenin's metaphor) just as fast as the Soviets, Mao saw this process as intimately linked to human change. And the connecting link between mass mobilization and technical revolution was to be provided by the slogan "Politics in command"—in other words, by unified Party leadership. The way in which the Party carried out its guiding role, however, involved a fundamental contradiction, for the dual rule re-introduced in 1956 was tilted so far in favour of the Party in 1958 that effective control at every level was vested in cadres who had no machinery at their disposal for checking, even if they had wanted to, on the wider consequences of their decisions. The result was fragmentation of economic initiative and control to such an extent that, as Mao later recognized, effective planning largely ceased to exist.

At the time, Mao suggested that this was nothing to worry about, since disequilibrium was a "universal objective law" which acted as a spur to

[32] *Wan-sui* (1969), p. 245; and *Wan-sui* (1967), p. 15.
[33] *Wan-sui* (1969), p. 204.

progress.[34] Back of this ideological formulation lay the conviction that it was imperative to mobilize the population as a whole to play a dynamic role in economic development. This, in turn, implied not only stressing the creativity of the masses, as opposed to the experts, but attributing to the "revolutionary people" as a whole (experts, or at least "red" experts among them) virtually unlimited capacities to modify their own environment. Thus we find, in ideological writings of the Great Leap period manifestly reflecting Mao's viewpoint, quite extraordinary statements such as "There is no such thing as poor land, but only poor methods for cultivating the land," or even "The subjective creates the objective."[35]

In the climate of euphoria which arose in China in the summer of 1958, utterly unrealistic visions were, as you all know, widely taken to constitute realistic expectations, or even accomplished fact. Summing up the situation in September 1958, Mao himself declared that the national grain output had more or less doubled, and might be expected to double again in 1959, so that soon there would be too much even to feed to the animals, and there would be a problem in disposing of it.[36]

During the ensuing years, the ambition of the Great Leap Forward to "overtake England in fifteen years," and the United States shortly thereafter, was soon revised in the direction of greater realism, but the ultimate aim was unchanged. Mao defined it, in January 1962, as carrying out, if possible in fifty years, more likely in a century, the industrial revolution which had required three hundred years in the capitalist countries of Europe. "China," he said, "has a large population, our resources are meagre, and our economy backward so that in my opinion it will be impossible to develop our productive power so rapidly as to catch up with, and overtake, the most advanced capitalist countries in less than one hundred years. If it requires only a few decades, for example only fifty years as some have conjectured, then that will be a splendid thing for which heaven and earth be praised."[37] In other words, if progress is slower, that will be the result of objective difficulties, and not of a deliberate policy choice.

In order to achieve this aim, effective coordination of efforts on a national scale would be required. In July 1959, in addition to expressing his regrets at what he had now come to regard as the ill-advised adventure of the backyard furnaces, Mao took responsibility for the dismantling of the planning system

[34]See S. Schram, "Mao Tse-tung and the Theory of the Permanent Revolution," *The China Quarterly*, April–June 1971, especially pp. 232–236.

[35]Wu Jiang 吳江, article in *Zhexue yanjiu* 哲學研究, no. 8, 1958, pp. 25–28; translated in S. Schram, *The Political Thought of Mao Tse-tung*, pp. 99, 135–136.

[36]*Wan-sui* (1969), p. 228.

[37]S. Schram, *Mao Tse-tung Unrehearsed*, pp. 174–175.

during the high tide of the Great Leap.

While accepting the need for more effective centralized control of the industrial sector, Mao took the lead in decentralizing ownership and control in the communes to the team level.[38] Probably he thought that, by himself recommending this measure, as he did in April 1959, he would disarm potential critics in the Party. As you all know, he did not succeed in this, and Peng Dehuai 彭德懷 openly attacked the whole range of Great Leap policies at the Lushan 廬山 Plenum of July-August 1959.

No other top leader supported Peng, though some figures of lesser rank did so, and Mao thus easily secured Peng's removal and disgrace. With the rest of the Party, an uneasy compromise was reached under which errors could be pointed out and corrected on a large scale, provided those involved did not say the basic policies had been wrong, and thus cast doubt on the quality of Mao's leadership.

On this basis, measures of rationalization and retrenchment were implemented in the early 1960s, and brought about a substantial degree of economic recovery. But as Mao watched this process, he became increasingly uneasy at the power wielded by the ministerial and managerial bureaucracy, at the emphasis on expertise to the neglect of redness, and above all at the appeal to material incentives in the countryside, through what later came to be known as the "sinister *sanzi yibao* 三自一包."

Unquestionably, he disliked these policies as such. But he disliked them even more because, without explicitly saying so, they appeared to amount to the wholesale repudiation of his own ideas of 1958, and thereby to constitute a blow to his image as the historic leader of the Chinese people. Perhaps the last straw was Liu Shaoqi's famous remark, at the January 1962 Work Conference: "When the Chairman says the situation is good, he means the political situation; the economic situation is very ungood (*da buhao* 大不好)."[39] Thereupon, Mao began to move steadily and relentlessly toward what was ultimately to become the greatest wave of all in what he had frequently called China's "wave-like pattern of advance": the Great Proletarian Cultural Revolution.

---

[38] *Wan-sui* (1967), pp. 104-115. What was called the team in 1959 was, in fact, the unit subsequently referred to as the brigade.

[39] *Guanyu Liu Shaoqi dang'an cailiao huibianji* 關於劉少奇檔案材料彙編集 (Tianjin 天津 : April 1967), pp. 26-28.

Questions and Answers

Q. Did Chairman Mao mention the relationship between his government during this period and the government of Qin Shihuang?

A. There are two dimensions to that question. One is the precise one of what he said about Qin Shihuang and that is linked to the *Pi-Lin* 批林 Campaign and the use made of those quotes in the 1960s and 1970s. Yes, indeed, at the Second Session of the Eighth Party Congress in May 1958 Mao did cite Qin Shihuang as a precursor. I will talk more about it tomorrow.

Your question also raises a general problem about Mao's feeling of continuity and "fellow feeling" with people who exercised the same *metier*, the same role, as China's previous rulers. At the Spring Forum on Education in February 1964, Mao made a couple of remarks. One was to say that the salary of Xuan Tong 宣統 the previous emperor, who was still alive, was not enough: "*Yibai duo yuan tai shaole, renjia shige huangdi*" (一百多元太少了，人家是個皇帝！).

This fellow's *jieji chengfen* 階級成分 or class status, was being an emperor, and a man whose *chengfen* was that of an emperor deserves a certain kind of treatment. In the same context Mao said that emperors Guang Xu 光緒 and Xuan Tong were "rulers under whom I have lived" (*wo dingtou shangsi* 我頂頭上司). I see in this reference to rulers under whom he had lived a hint on Mao's part that he perceived himself as in some sense their successor—but I prefer to leave further discussion of Mao's last years until tomorrow.

Q. In 1959, there was a very serious food crisis in China that lasted until approximately 1961. Did Mao believe that the food crisis between 1959 and 1961 was a famine? What impact did this serious food crisis have on Mao's policy after 1962?

A. Although he was sitting in Beijing and people would neglect to tell him things that were unpleasant to hear, this famine was so patently obvious that he had to know it. I stressed that many people died during the period following the Great Leap in my article in *The China Quarterly* last September, and how harshly Mao was criticized for that. The famine damaged the morale of the People's Liberation Army, which from 1960 onward was the main pillar of Mao's power. When the soldiers would go back to their home villages and find that Granny had starved to death they would be in a very bad mood when they rejoined their units, and you can read about this in the *Work Bulletin* 工作通訊 of the Liberation

Army. These events affected his attitude very much between 1959 and 1962. Hence Mao was prepared to backtrack, provided he could save some face, and it was not said straight out that the Great Leap was a disaster. In the course of the year 1962, the economic situation improved somewhat, thanks to the "sinister *sanzi yibao* 三自一包" promoted by Liu Shaoqi and others. The impact of the crisis on Mao's behaviour faded away in 1962, and he began to think it was time to push forward once again. His memory should have been longer. It might have been better for him and for the Chinese people if his memory had been longer, but he was an impetuous man who shook off one impression quickly and moved on to something else, and having compromised and accepted a playing-down and even a repudiation of his policies, he then lashed back. In some respects, the current Chinese criticism of the Great Leap is more significant in the overall evaluation of Mao than the criticism of the Cultural Revolution.

Q. It has been suggested that to talk about "democratic centralism," is like saying *guomindang de gongchandang* 國民黨的共產黨 or *gongchandang de guomindang* 共產黨的國民黨, i.e., putting two contradictory terms together. Somebody has spoken of this as a form of hypocrisy, and I think that this criticism has been raised not only by non-Marxists but also by some Marxists including Antonio Gramsci. I am sure that there must be some people who feel that we should give this concept the benefit of the doubt. The failure of Mao Zedong in China does not necessarily negate the value of democratic centralism. Do you have any additional comments to make on this?

A. Yes, I can make a few additional comments. First of all, when you say that the failure of this concept in China doesn't need to put us off this concept altogether, I think it must be acknowledged that the Chinese interpretation, which was the Maoist interpretation of democratic centralism is in fact more open, flexible and democratic than that in any other Communist Party I know of. Lenin, after all, invented the term to apply not to society as a whole, or to patterns of rule in society as a whole, but simply to relations between upper and lower levels in the party itself, and to how the party functions. This is still the way the Soviets use it. Lenin's interpretation was, in essence, you can discuss anything in the cells provided you don't say anything outside, and provided that you don't insist on your own views as an intellectual. There is theoretically a pyramid of elections up to the top. In fact, the thrust of authority in the party essentially comes from the top down. There is discussion at the lower levels, but only until a decision has been taken, and then everyone must implement that decision and that's it. I don't know whether this

conception of democratic centralism, as modified in the Chinese interpretations, will prove viable in the future. Certainly the Soviet interpretation cannot persist unchanged, or at least I hope not.

Secondly, putting two contradictory concepts together is not
necessarily meaningless. Mao, or any Marxist or Hegelian sees reality as a
tissue of contradictions and believes that everything consists of contradictory elements. However you formulate it, this question of maintaining
some degree of order and consensus in society while at the same time
allowing a certain amount of freedom of choice for the individual and
individual initiative is in fact a universal problem. I am not suggesting that
the Chinese are as near to a solution or that the Soviets are as near to a
solution as Western democracies, but I am simply saying that it is a universal problem. There is an existential contradiction that is not easily resolved.

Q. You just mentioned that none of the leaders supported Peng Dehuai in
his criticism of Mao. I have the impression that there was a very painful
showdown. Did Mao ever level a serious threat, or was it just the appre-
hension of the other leaders that he would?

A. What I meant was that no one really stuck his neck out. Zhou Xiaozhou
周小舟 and Huang Kecheng 黃克誠 did, and were not able to resist Mao.
Zhang Wentian 張聞天 did indicate his support for Peng. Neither Liu
Shaoqi nor Zhou Enlai nor the others pressed it into a confrontation
with Mao. Roderick MacFarquhar has written in the second volume of
his trilogy on the origins of the Cultural Revolution a chapter entitled
"High Noon at Lushan." That is a very good title, although perhaps a bit
journalistic. There really was a kind of shoot-out at the OK Corral. When
it came to the crunch, intimidated, whether by Mao's mutterings that he
would go to recruit peasants for a new Red army in the countryside, or
simply by knowing that Mao was a vengeful sort of character, none of
the top leadership, among the top half-dozen or so, stuck his neck out
to support Peng, though a number of them were probably in private
agreement with him.

Q. How did Mao react to the denunciation of Stalin in Russia during the
twentieth Congress of the Communist Party?

A. Mao's feelings about Stalin were plainly very ambiguous. On the one
hand he had suffered under Stalin. On the other hand, Stalin was the
leader of the world communist movement for roughly the first 30 years
of Mao's own participation in it. Mao at one point remarked that it is
very hard to be the son of a patriarchal father. It was very hard to live
with a leader like that. And apart from the ambiguity of his own feelings
about Stalin there was of course a question about the use that might be
made in China of any deStalinization, or the parallels that might be

drawn and the criticism of Mao's own cult that might ensue. First of all, he was thoroughly aware that Stalin had committed a number of errors. This was said officially for the first time in 1963, I believe, in the second of the nine replies of the Chinese to the Soviets. On the question of Stalin they said to Khrushchev, "You don't have to tell us that Stalin committed errors. Long ago we Chinese Communists suffered from those errors." The situation was extremely difficult for Mao, given that from 1958 onwards, he increasingly considered Khrushchev an unreliable ally, someone who made fun of China's communes. If you are going to denounce Khrushchev as a revisionist, then you have to have someone as a foil for Khrushchev. You can't say that everything in the Soviet Union since Lenin was a mess, and you have to defend Stalin for that reason. They are still defending Stalin in China today, at least in public, because Stalin is a symbol for not accepting the Khrushchevite line, the revisionist line or the "social imperialist" line in the Soviet Union. From 1955 onward Mao criticized Stalin for his treatment of the peasants. For example, Mao said in April 1956, "We mustn't treat the peasants too badly or we will have the dead cattle problem on our hands," in other words, the problem of the peasants slaughtering their cattle to eat them rather than keeping them to work for the collective. "Stalin made a shambles of collectivization, we must not duplicate that." He also criticized Stalin as a philosopher, for being undialectical, and in various other respects, but he was reluctant to see Stalin cut down to size, publicly, first of all, because of the need for a symbol against Khrushchev. The issue of the personality cult and one-man rule was a delicate problem for him in China as well. In the first volume of MacFarquhar's book, he writes about the Eighth Congress and the speeches by Deng Xiaoping and Liu Shaoqi in a way that accords with my perception, namely that Deng Xiaoping went into this question at some length in a way which was designed to protect Mao. He said, "We all revere Chairman Mao but we revere him because he stands for the truth and because he is the leader of the party not as an individual." But none the less the elimination of Mao's Thought from the Communist Party constitution or the party statutes adopted in 1956 and these first moves toward a criticism of the personality cult in the Communist Party of China had worried Mao. These are two reasons why the Chinese subsequently have not gone farther in their criticism of Stalin. They may in the future; I don't have any advance knowledge, but the logic of events might lead them to do so.

Q. Are there any figures in the Chinese past whom Mao generally admired and whose political ideas or strategies he used in his struggles?

A. Of figures in the Chinese past, he admired strong rulers. He admired a lot of people who were classified as Legalists back in 1972 to 1975, but he was not so silly and crude as to stick the label "Legalist" on them. He knew perfectly well that from Han times onward it was meaningless to speak of a philosopher or statesman as a Confucian or a Legalist. The people he mentioned in a favourable context on the whole are people esteemed by the statecraft, *jingshi* 經世 school from the seventeenth to the nineteenth centuries. He admired a lot of people from the Chinese past, mainly this kind, and of course he admired great rebels of every description.

I suggested in an article published last September that Mao tried to combine the little and great traditions, being at once the emperor and the rebel, and gloried in this ambiguous and on the whole retrograde symbolic role. As for his contemporaries, quite obviously he had very great respect for Zhou Enlai as a master workman in government and in diplomacy. Exactly what the personal relations between Mao and Zhou were like, I don't know. I think that Mao regarded himself, especially after 1949, and more especially after 1959, as above everyone else. I can't think of anyone offhand whom he intensely admired.

Q. How about Lu Xun and Chiang Kaishek?

A. Lu Xun, certainly, although the interpretation that was put forward in the 1970s and even Mao's interpretation was a bit one-sided. For Chiang Kaishek I don't think he ever had a high regard. When he was co-operating with the Guomindang he had to say the Guomindang had two great leaders—Mr. Sun Yatsen 孫逸仙 and Mr. Chiang Kaishek. It is not all that certain that he had all that much respect for Sun Yatsen either. He made certain to express a great deal of admiration, but in one speech around 1960, or in the late 1950s, he says that Sun Yatsen was not all that democratic in that he wanted to run everything himself and that as far as theory was concerned he was all water and no bone—no substance.

In Mao's youth he had admiration for many people—on the one hand for Zeng Guofan and on the other for Li Dazhao, and Cai Yuanpei 蔡元培 and other leading figures of the May Fourth Movement. But I suppose that your question concerns the sort of people that Mao admired as a ruler during the 1950s and 1960s. De Gaulle is one such figure. There isn't any doubt about it at all. To one of the first French parliamentary delegations to Beijing in early 1964, before the first French ambassador had even arrived but after relations had been re-established, Mao said about de Gaulle that "from the top of his head to the soles of his feet he's a military man. I, too, am a military man." Mao said he admired de Gaulle just as, among the figures from French revolutionary days, he most admired Napoleon.

He admired de Gaulle enormously because he saw de Gaulle's role and his policies as similar to his own. He was number two in the capitalist camp and was thumbing his nose at number one. And Mao was in the same position; he was number two in the socialist camp and he was thumbing his nose at the number one power. On all kinds of grounds de Gaulle was good.

Q. Nixon also admired de Gaulle without limits. What were Mao Zedong's thoughts on Nixon?

A. He seems to have had more admiration for him than I do.

Q. In his memoires, Khrushchev refers to a conversation he had with Mao in 1957. Khrushchev may or may not be regarded as a reliable witness, but he said that when Mao spoke about the top leadership in the Chinese Communist Party, he spoke very critically about most people, but he spoke about one man very favourably, and that was Deng Xiaoping 鄧小平.

A. Yes, in fact their relations were very good. One hears such reports from all sides. In fact as late as December of 1975, while talking to President Ford, Mao indicated that Deng was his successor.

Q. You mentioned earlier that few members of the Chinese Communist Party had read Marx in the original. Liu Shaoqi also wrote that Mao did not read Marx in the original.

A. In the course of the power struggle between Mao and Wang Ming and the Twenty-Eight Bolsheviks in the 1920s, and as late as 1941, Liu Shaoqi had not decided in which direction to jump. In March 1943 Mao was elected Chairman and in July Liu wrote the first of a series of articles making it known that Mao was a great theoretician and the leader of the Communist Party. I put in the reference to Liu's letter of 1941 to Sun Yefang not to show that there was always a struggle between two lines and that Liu was a revisionist element, but to show that the alliance between the two still hadn't been sealed. In my opinion Liu and Mao were very different men not only in personality but also in experience. Liu, in the 1920s, 30s and 40s was of course working in the white areas in the cities. In their background and mentality Mao and Liu were very different. They sealed some kind of alliance in 1942 or 1943, and for twenty years that alliance maintained stability in China. In the early 1960s the alliance broke up and all hell broke loose. That is a very simplified formulation, but something like that happened. In 1941 the alliance had not yet been concluded and Liu Shaoqi made this remark, which must have been to some extent an attack on Mao. Anyway, he was putting things in a way that was not to Mao's glory.

Q. The responsibility farm system was first experimented with in 1962. Was

Mao aware of this in January 1962, and had he already been briefed at
that time, making it possible for him to use the *sanzi yibao* to criticize
Liu Shaoqi?

A.   You are obviously right that in January 1962 Mao could not already have
     been preoccupied with the *sanzi yibao*. He was preoccupied with a
     resurgence of an emphasis on material inventives, of which the *sanzi
     yibao* later became the symbol in the Cultural Revolution polemics. My
     point, however, was that it was sometime in 1962, perhaps in the after-
     math of the 7,000-cadre meeting, that Mao decided that enough was
     enough in terms of policies that appeared to disavow his Great Leap.

Professor T. C. Chen: Yelü Chucai 耶律楚材, a prime minister to the
     Mongols once made a very famous remark. Apparently he saved the
     Chinese cities by telling Ghenghis Khan that you can take the country on
     a horse but you cannot rule the country from horseback. Presumably
     Ghenghis Khan took his advice and decided not to convert the city of
     Peking into a pasture for his cowherd. The impression I got listening to
     Professor Schram was that in this second stage of Mao Zedong's career he
     was most comfortable when he was fighting for his life. During the first
     stage of his life he was able to hold the party together and led a successful
     revolution to take over the country. In the second stage he was not quite
     able to gain the kind of respect that he felt was due him and perhaps he
     also decided to experiment on his political and economic theories—
     some of which seem to have backfired. It therefore appears logical that
     there should be a third lecture. If one cannot rule on a horse, can one
     rule on a pedestal? The third lecture tomorrow will be "From Apotheosis
     to Oblivion," with a question mark. Professor Schram insisted on this
     question mark, leaving us to wonder what he really will tell us—we leave
     this question mark until tomorrow.

The Final Phase: From Apotheosis to Oblivion?

The titles of my first two lectures were more or less descriptive and matter-of-fact. This one is more provocative. The question mark at the end of it applies, of course, to the last word, and not to the title as a whole. That the Cultural Revolution decade saw a kind of apotheosis of Mao Zedong and his thought is not subject to doubt. The question raised by the title is a two-fold one: Is Mao already on the road to oblivion as a result of the actions of the current Chinese leadership? And is he fated, in any case, to be consigned ultimately to oblivion by history?

In approaching these questions, I shall begin by examining some trends which emerged in Mao Zedong's thinking during the 1960s. I have selected the year 1962 as the dividing-line between this phase and the previous one because it seems to me that there was, to use Mao's own vocabulary, a "qualitative leap" in his general outlook and political stance between early 1962, when he made on the whole an extremely moderate and balanced speech at the "7000 cadres conference," and August-September 1962, when he put forward the call "Never forget the class struggle!" But in order to put this brusque (or apparently brusque) mutation in proper perspective, it is necessary to go back a bit, and to trace the appearance on Mao's part, during the years 1958-1962, of an increasingly acute concern with the problem of "new bourgeois elements," and related phenomena in Chinese society.

Mao's approach to these matters had deep roots in the past, in the memories of the austerity and spirit of sacrifice which had characterized the twenty years of struggle in the countryside. In April 1969, he declared:

> For years we did not have any such thing as salaries. We had no eight-tier wage system. We had only a fixed amount of food, three mace of oil and five of salt. If we got 1½ catties of millet, that was great. . . . Now we have entered the cities. This is a good thing. If we hadn't entered the cities Chiang Kai-shek would be occupying them. But it is also a bad thing because it caused our Party to deteriorate.[1]

Despite the existence of a few passages such as this reflecting an actual nostalgia for the heroic days of the past, Mao quite evidently did not imagine

---

[1] *Mao Tse-tung Unrehearsed*, p. 288.

that it was possible to go back to the world of the Jinggangshan, or wish to do so. He was determined, however, that the values of the past should be preserved in forms appropriate to the new conditions. Consequently, he did not wish to adopt policies which, though effective in the short run, might create institutions or attitudes which would inhibit the move toward communism when the time was ripe.

A crucial turning point in Mao's thinking regarding these matters was marked by the generational change in China's educated elite which took place in the latter half of 1957. As I noted in yesterday's lecture, Mao had believed during the "Hundred Flowers" period that technical and managerial cadres inherited from the old society could, despite their bourgeois origins, be made red as well as expert, and their loyalty gained. When these hopes proved unjustified, he began to place the emphasis on training a new generation of intellectuals whose redness was not open to doubt.

This generational change was directly related to the problem of salaries and material incentives, for it had long been accepted that, because they were accustomed to a certain standard of living, the "old" intellectuals must be paid high salaries. Mao himself had defended, in January 1957, what he called "buying over" at a "small cost" the capitalists plus the democrats and intellectuals associated with them.[2] Obviously the same considerations did not apply to the newly-trained young people, who did not have such expensive tastes, and who might be assumed to have a higher level of political consciousness.

In the atmosphere of euphoria which reigned in the autumn of 1958, when Mao and many others were persuaded that grain production could be made to double every year for the indefinite future, many communes abolished or diminished the role of workpoints, and instituted a free supply system for grain and other essential foodstuffs. One of those who set out to draw theoretical conclusions from this situation (or from what they imagined to be the situation) was none other than Zhang Chunqiao 張春橋.

In an article entitled "Smash and Eliminate the Ideology of Bourgeois Right," published in September in Shanghai and reprinted on 13 October, 1958 in *People's Daily*, Zhang asserted that, before Liberation, "a pattern of military-communist life, characterized by the 'free supply system'" had enjoyed favour, and been regarded as glorious. After 1949, many young people, too, had looked up to this tradition, but very soon it had been supplanted by an emphasis on material incentives corresponding to "the ideology of bourgeois right." The resulting inequalities, which found concrete expression in the "grade level system," could not be eliminated overnight, but they

[2] *Selected Works*, V, p. 395.

should, Zhang argued, be kept to a minimum, and phased out as soon as possible.

People's Daily carried an introductory note to this article which some have attributed to Mao. If the Chairman did write it, his endorsement was not unqualified. Zhang's article, the note said, was "basically correct," and presented the question "clearly and vividly," in a "popular" style "easy to understand." But on the other hand, it gave an "incomplete explanation of the historical process," and was therefore "one-sided in certain respects." If Mao found the article lacking in historical perspective, it is no doubt because Zhang wanted to restrict the scope of bourgeois right very quickly, so that cadres and masses would shortly be living and toiling together as in the heroic days of the past. Mao himself declared in his speech of November 1958 on Stalin's *Economic Problems of Socialism in the USSR* that it was necessary to smash and eliminate certain aspects of the "ideology of bourgeois right," such as "putting on airs like overlords," and "bearing or appearance unlike that of ordinary working people." But at the same time he stressed that the grade level system could not be eliminated too rapidly, and added:

> Commodity circulation, commodity form, and the law of value cannot . . . be demolished at one blow, although they also belong to the domain of the bourgeoisie. At present, we are promoting the idea of smashing and eliminating the whole ideology of bourgeois right; . . . the way it is being put now is inappropriate.[3]

A year or two later, Mao began to see things differently, as a result of his discovery of the "new class." Previously, Mao had always defined the threat from "enemy classes" primarily in terms of the surviving influence of the privileged strata of the old society. Now he began to interpret boureaucratic tendencies no longer simply as a defect in work style, but as the manifestation of a change in the class character of the Party. Not surprisingly, some of his earliest comments on this theme occur in his reading notes of 1960 on the Soviet textbook of political economy, since in his view this process of degeneration had begun earlier and was farther advanced in Russia. "Although a socialist society has abolished classes," he wrote, "in the process of its development it will probably have certain problems with 'vested interest groups'." Such people, he said, were all too happy with the existing system, and therefore opposed the transition to more advanced patterns of distribution.[4]

Regarding incentives, Mao's position had consistently been that politics, and individual or group self-interest should be combined. Thus in February

[3] *Wan-sui* (1967), pp. 117–118.
[4] *Ibid.*, p. 192.

1959, when the egalitarian "wind of communism" was blowing in the Chinese countryside, Mao declared that the share of individual ownership was too small, and did not accord with the principle of material incentives. Politics could not be underestimated, he said, but 70 per cent politics and 30 per cent material incentives was too high a proportion.[5] In 1960, however, in his comments on the Soviet textbook, Mao began to put the emphasis differently:

> Even if one acknowledges that material incentive is an important principle, it absolutely cannot be the only principle. There must always be another principle— the principle of spiritual incentives in the political and ideological domain. At the same time, material incentives cannot be discussed merely in terms of individual interests, one must also talk about collective interests, and about subordinating individual interests to collective interests . . . , and partial interests to the interests of the whole.[6]

These texts refer only to "interests," or at most to "interest groups." It was, to my knowledge, in his speech of 30 January, 1962 that Mao first referred to the possibility that in a socialist society "new bourgeois elements may still be produced." This was in the context of the famous passage asserting that "during the whole socialist stage there still exist classes and class struggle, and this class struggle is a protracted, complex, and sometimes even violent affair," and stressing the need to struggle against the surviving remnants of the old reactionary classes, which were "still planning a comeback."[7] Nevertheless, the suggestion that bourgeois elements of a new type could emerge from within the socialist system itself, although it was only thrown out in passing, was ultimately to have dramatic consequences.

In August 1962, at a preliminary meeting of the Central Committee in Beidaihe 北戴河 , Mao revised the conclusion which he himself had drawn in 1955 regarding classes in Chinese society: "In the book *Socialist Upsurge in China's Countryside* [edited by Mao] there is an annotation saying that the bourgeoisie has been eliminated, and only the influence of the remnants of bourgeois ideology remains. This is wrong, and should be corrected. . . . The bourgeoisie can be born anew; such a situation exists in the Soviet Union."[8] And at the formal Tenth Plenum in the following month, Mao put forward the slogan "Never forget the class struggle!"

I have suggested in the synopsis of these lectures that in Mao's later years, certain pairs of opposites which had hitherto co-existed in dynamic and creative tension became dissociated, thus unleashing forces that ultimately propelled his thought and action into destructive channels. In several crucial

[5] *Ibid.*, pp. 18-19.
[6] *Ibid.*, pp. 206, 210.
[7] *Mao Tse-tung Unrehearsed*, p. 168.
[8] *Wan-sui* (1969), p. 424.

and interrelated respects, this unravelling of the previous synthesis began with the Tenth Plenum. Increasingly, Mao came to perceive the relation between the leaders, with their privileges, and the rest of society, as an antagonistic contradiction rather than a contradiction among the people. The consequence which inevitably flowed from this insight was that the Party, considered as an entity which included virtually all of these privileged power-holders, must be not simply tempered and purified in contact with the masses, but smashed, at least in large part.

On 20 December, 1964, Mao castigated those "power-holders" among the cadres who were primarily concerned about getting more wage points for themselves, and said that the "hat" of "new bourgeois elements" should be stuck on "particularly vicious offenders" among them. He warned, however, against overestimating their number, and said they should be referred to as elements or cliques, not as "strata"—still less, obviously, as a fully-formed class.[9] On 27 December, 1964, he indicated that there were "at least two factions" in the Chinese Communist Party, a socialist faction and a capitalist faction, and that these two factions incarnated the principal contradiction in Chinese society.[10] The following day, 28 December, Mao opened a "Central Work Conference" by laying on the table his 23-article directive for the "Socialist Education Campaign," of which the crucial point was "to rectify those in authority in the Party taking the capitalist road," and said abruptly: "I don't have much to say. Is this document acceptable or isn't it?"[11] The clash with those in the leadership who found such a directive unacceptable was henceforth inevitable.

Apart from the relation between the Party, or privileged elements in the Party, and the masses, two other polarities which became dissociated in Mao's thinking in the early 1960s were that of material and moral incentives, and that of professional knowledge and the creativity of the masses. In a word, whereas Mao had stressed, as late as 1959 and even 1960, the need to combine moral and material incentives, the latter were progressively subordinated to the former, and then condemned altogether as revisionist and immoral. And yet it was precisely on the masses of the population, who were deprived of material incentives (except to a very limited extent, in collective rather than individual form) that Mao proposed to rely in building a socialist economy, instead of, rather than in addition to, the experts.

It is not surprising that, in these circumstances, Mao should have been gripped by increasing pessimism, to the point where he came to feel that the continuing forward march of the revolution was something of a miracle,

[9]*Ibid.*, pp. 582-588.
[10]*Ibid.*, pp. 597-598.
[11]*Ibid.*, p. 598.

against the grain of history, rather than the inevitable consequence of the unfolding logic of economic development. For if progress depended primarily on the virtue of the masses, it would always be at the mercy of the "bourgeois" attitudes lurking in the hearts even of workers, peasants, and veteran revolutionaries. Only unending struggle could triumph over the tendency toward human backsliding. And unending struggle is, of course, what Mao sought to launch, and indeed to institutionalize, in the course of the Cultural Revolution. But before turning to the last decade of Mao's life, I want to comment on the significance of the unravelling of another polarity in Mao Zedong's thought of the early 1960s—that between Marxism and the Chinese tradition.

Two familiar texts bracket and sum up the shift in Mao's position between the mid-1950s and the mid-1960s in this respect. In the first of these, the "Talk to Music Workers" of August 1956, Mao adopted the relatively balanced view he had expounded since 1938, namely that China must learn many things from the West, while remaining herself. On the one hand, he said: "We learn foreign things because we want to study and develop Chinese things." But at the same time, he explicitly rejected Zhang Zhidong's *ti-yong* 體用 formula, saying:

> Some people advocate "Chinese learning as the substance, Western learning for practical application." Is this idea right or wrong? It is wrong. The word "learning" in fact refers to fundamental theory. . . . Marxism is a fundamental theory which was produced in the West. How then can we make a distinction between what is Chinese and what is Western in this respect? . . . Marxism is a general truth which has universal application. We must accept it. But this general truth must be combined with the concrete practice of each nation's revolution. . . . [12]

In December 1965, in his speech at Hangzhou 杭州, Mao Zedong reversed his attitude toward the *ti-yong* formula, saying in effect that Zhang Zhidong was right:

> The substance was like our General Line, which cannot be changed. We cannot adopt Western learning as the substance, nor can we use the substance of the democratic republic. We cannot use "the natural rights of man" nor the "theory of evolution." We can only use Western technology. [13]

On a philosophical level, Mao sounded in 1960, in his reading notes on the Soviet textbook of political economy, notes which are scarcely to be found in the Marxist tradition. Commenting on the phrase "Consolidate completely the system of collective farms," he wrote:

> When I read these two words "consolidate completely" I feel ill at ease. The consolidation of anything is relative; how can it be complete? If, since the human

---

[12] *Mao Tse-tung Unrehearsed*, pp. 85-86.
[13] *Ibid.*, pp. 234-235.

race has existed, all men had not died, but had been "completely consolidated," what would this world be like? . . .

Socialism will definitely pass over to communism, and at the time of transition to a communist society, some things from the socialist stage will certainly die. In the communist period, too, there will also be uninterrupted development. . . .[14]

Some perspectives of this kind had been opened by Mao in 1958, when he wrote in his directive on the permanent revolution that even when the era of communism had been reached, there would still be many stages linked by mutations amounting to "revolutions," and involving struggle. He had also shown something then of the acceptance of human mortality expressed in the first paragraph of the above quotation. In the mid-1960s, however, this note became more insistent, and was accompanied by explicit references to the Taoist classics. "I approve of Zhuangzi's 莊子 approach," he said in 1964. "When his wife died, he banged on a basin and sang. When people die, there should be parties to celebrate the victory of the dialectics, to celebrate the destruction of the old."[15]

While this Olympian detachment is characteristic of Mao Zedong, especially in his later years, it should not be taken to imply any lessening of his determination to press forward with the revolution. On the contrary, in the very passage just quoted, Mao went on to say that the difference between his outlook and that of classical Marxism might be found in a greater emphasis on the need for men to strive actively to make their own history:

Engels spoke of moving from the realm of necessity to the realm of freedom, and said that freedom is the understanding of necessity. This sentence is not complete, it only says one half and leaves the rest unsaid. Does merely understanding it make you free? Freedom is the understanding of necessity and the transformation of necessity—one has some work to do too. . . . When you discover a law, you must be able to apply it, you must create the world anew, you must break the ground and edify buildings, you must dig mines, industrialize. In the future there will be more people, and there won't be enough grain, so men will have to get food from minerals. Thus it is that only by transformation can freedom be obtained. Will it be possible in the future to be all that free? . . .[16]

The notion of "creating the world anew" by industrializing is, of course, a Promethean goal wholly in keeping with the Leninist approach to building socialism. Mao's query as to whether man will be "all that free" even under communism reflects, however, an unusual scepticism, and in other texts of the early 1960s, he expressed even deeper doubts as to whether the forward march of the revolution would be continued, and whether communism would ever be reached.

[14] *Wan-sui* (1967), pp. 186-187.
[15] *Mao Tse-tung Unrehearsed*, p. 227.
[16] *Ibid.*, p. 228.

One curious consequence of Mao's rediscovery of Taoism (and also of Buddhism) in 1964 was his abandonment of two of the "three categories" of Marxist dialectics, including the negation of the negation. In 1958 he had explicitly reaffirmed these, saying: "The law of the unity of opposites, the law of quantitative and qualitative change, the law of affirmation and negation, exist forever and universally."[17] Now he declared that he "did not believe" in the last two. The transformation of quality and quantity into one another, he said, was merely a special case of the unity of opposites, and he denied the existence of the negation of the negation altogether.[18]

By arguing that "every link in the chain of events is both affirmation and negation," Mao could be held to have seriously undermined the whole Marxist and Hegelian justification, in philosophical terms, for the idea that history moves irreversibly forward. As I suggested a moment ago, the roots of Mao's anxiety regarding the future of the revolution are no doubt to be found primarily in his evaluation of the situation prevailing in the early 1960s, but this abandonment of the Hegelian paradigm of thesis-antithesis-synthesis may well have contributed to his feeling of uncertainty.

Thus the stage was set for the Cultural Revolution. At the outset of this upheaval, it was the radical calling into question of the Party, and indeed of authority in all its forms, which attracted the most attention. In retrospect, it is clear that Mao's repudiation of leadership from above was not so sweeping as it appeared at the time. Nevertheless, he did go very far.

In his comments of 1960 on the Soviet manual, Mao had declared: "No matter what, we cannot regard history as the creation of the planners, it is the creation of the masses."[19] And yet, he had always held, down to the eve of the Cultural Revolution, the view that the masses could exercise this role of making history only if they benefited from correct leadership. As the great confrontation with the Party approached, in the summer of 1965, he went a step farther, proclaiming that democracy meant "dealing with the affairs of the masses through the masses themselves." There were, he added, two lines: to rely entirely on a few individuals, and to mobilize the masses. "Democratic politics," he said, "must rely on everyone running things, not on a minority of people running things." At the same time, however, he called once more for reliance on "the leadership of the Party at the higher level and on the broad masses at the lower level."[20] It was only with the actual onset of the Cultural Revolution, in March 1966, that Mao sounded a much more radical

[17] "Sixty Articles on Work Methods," par. 22; my translation, from *The China Quarterly*, no. 46 (1971), p. 228. But see the Preface.
[18] *Mao Tse-tung Unrehearsed*, p. 226.
[19] *Wan-sui* (1967), p. 206.
[20] *Wan-sui*, p. 30.

note, suggesting that the masses could dispense with centralized Party leadership:

> ... The Propaganda Department of the Central Committee is the palace of the King of Hell. We must overthrow the palace of the King of Hell and set the little devils free. I have always advocated that whenever the central organs do bad things, it is necessary to call upon the localities to rebel, and to attack the centre. The localities must produce many Sun Wukongs 孫悟空 to create a great disturbance in the palace of the King of Heaven. ... [21]

Two months later, these "Monkey Kings" burst upon the scene, using Mao's own rhetoric, including the slogan "To rebel is justified!" which he had coined in 1939, attributing it—irony of ironies—to Stalin.[22] "Daring to ... rebel is ... the fundamental principle of the proletarian Party spirit," proclaimed the Red Guards of Qinghua 清華 University Middle School. "Revolutionaries are Monkey Kings. ... We wield our golden rods, display our supernatural powers, and use our magic to turn the old world upside down, smash it to pieces, pulverize it and create chaos—the greater the confusion the better! We are bent on creating a tremendous proletarian uproar, and hewing out a proletarian new world!"[23] The "old world" these Red Guards wanted to smash was, of course, that controlled by the Party; they did not propose to rectify it, but to dissolve it in the chaos of the Cultural Revolution, and replace it by a completely new order.

Mao himself never prolcaimed such a goal. At a Central Work Conference on 23 August, he remarked, "The principal question is what policy we should adopt regarding the so-called disturbances [suowei luan 所謂亂] in various areas. My view is that we should let disorder reign for a few months [luan ta jige yue 亂他幾個月] .... Even if there are no provincial Party committees, it doesn't matter; aren't there still district and xian committees?"[24]

The phrase "for a few months" should probably be taken literally, to mean three or four months, or six at the outside. That in itself would have made the Cultural Revolution more like a conventional rectification campaign. Nevertheless, by accepting the prospect that for a time the Party might survive only in the form of local-level committees, the central organs having been effectively smashed and put out of action, Mao was at the very least taking the risk of destroying the political instrument to which he had devoted more than four decades of his life, in order to purge it of his enemies.

---

[21] Wan-sui (1969), p. 640.

[22] Mao Zedong ji, Vol. 7, p. 142; translated in The Political Thought of Mao Tse-tung, pp. 427–428.

[23] Renmin ribao 人民日報 , 24 August, 1966; translated in Peking Review, no. 37, 1966, pp. 2-21.

[24] Wan-sui (1969), p. 653.

When events moved in such a direction, in late 1966 and early 1967, that the threat to the very existence of the Party became acute, Mao was forced to choose between Leninism and anarchy. He had no hesitation in preferring the former. Speaking in February 1967 to Zhang Chunqiao and Yao Wenyuan 姚文元, Mao noted that some people in Shanghai had demanded the abolition of "heads," and commented: "This is extreme anarchism, it is most reactionary. If instead of calling someone the 'head' of something, we call him 'orderly' or 'assistant,' this would really be only a formal change. In reality, there will still always be heads."[25] Discussing the objections to setting up communes as organs of government, as Zhang and Yao had just done in Shanghai, Mao queried: "Where will we put the Party? . . . In a commune there has to be a party; can the commune replace the party?"[26] The history of the ensuing nine years made it abundantly clear that in the Chairman's view it could not.

Indeed, having rejected, after only the briefest hesitation, in the winter of 1966-1967, the "Paris Commune" model Mao Zedong moved, during the ensuing decade, toward the imposition of a centralizing and authoritarian vision which owed less to Marx, or even to Stalin, than to the Chinese tradition. And yet, at the time when this tendency, symbolized by the veritable cult of Qin Shihuang, was at its height in the early 1970s, those whom Mao allowed to speak in his name, such as Zhang Chunqiao and Yao Wenyuan, promoted simultaneously radical egalitarian ideas with a Marxist colouration, under the slogan of the "Abolition of Bourgeois Right." Here is a further example of the unravelling of the synthesis between Marxism and Chinese culture which merits reflection.

As I noted yesterday, Mao, who had denounced teachers of Chinese literature in 1919 as "obstinate pendants" who "forcibly impregnate our minds with a lot of stinking corpse-like dead writings full of classical allusions,"[27] had come to take the view, by 1938, that the classical heritage had a positive as well as a negative aspect, and that it was therefore necessary to deal selectively with it. On the one hand, he had no more doubts than he had ever had since the May 4th period about the reactionary and harmful character of Confucianism as an answer to the problems of the twentieth century. But at the same time, from the 1930s to the 1950s, he alluded with approval to various attitudes defined by tags from the Confucian classics, such as Confucius' practice of going about and "enquiring into everything,"[28] his attitude

[25]*Mao Tse-tung Unrehearsed*, p. 277.

[26]*Wan-sui* (1969), pp. 670-671.

[27]"The Great Union of the Popular Masses"; my translation, from *The China Quarterly*, no. 49 (1972), pp. 80-81.

[28]"Oppose Book Worship," in *Selected Readings* (Beijing: Foreign Languages Press, 1967), p. 34. (*Analects* VII, 2; Legge, p. 195.)

of "not feeling ashamed to ask and learn from people below,"[29] and the recommendation from the *Mencius*: "When speaking to the mighty, look on them with contempt."[30]

In 1959, Mao remarked: "There are some things which need not have any national style, such as trains, airplanes, and big guns. Politics and art should have a national style."[31]

It was in 1964, however, that Mao's turn back to the Chinese classics for inspiration led him not only to the fascination with Taoist dialectics which I discussed a moment ago, but to a surprisingly favourable view of Confucius. While criticizing the Sage for his contempt for manual labour, and for his lack of interest in agriculture, Mao declared in February 1964, at the Spring Forum on Education:

> Confucius was from a poor peasant family; he herded sheep, and never attended middle school or university either. . . . In his youth, he came from the masses, and understood something of the suffering of the masses. Later, he became an official in the state of Lu 魯 , though not a terribly high official. . . .[32]

The following August, in his philosophical conversations with Kang Sheng and Chen Boda 陳伯達 , Mao quoted with approval a passage from the *Shi Jing* 詩經 , commenting: "This is a poem which accuses heaven and opposes the rulers. Confucius, too, was rather democratic. . . ."[33]

These indulgent assessments should obviously not be taken as Mao's last word on the subject, since it was only two years later that he launched the Great Proletarian Cultural Revolution, directed against the "Four Olds," in other words, against the imprint of Confucianism on the patterns of thought and behaviour of the Chinese people. They do make plain, however, just how far from the mainstream of Mao's thinking on these matters were some of the interpretations put forward during the years 1973-1975.

The same is true of the great positive symbol of the *pi-Lin pi-Kong* 批林 批孔 Campaign. In a famous passage from one of his speeches to the Second Session of the Eight Party Congress in May 1958, Mao had hailed Qin Shihuang, the first Qin emperor, as a "specialist in stressing the present and slighting the past," quoting with approval Li Si's 李斯 proposal, endorsed by the emperor, that "those who make use of the past to disparage the present should be exterminated together with their whole families [*Yi gu fei jin zhe zu* 以古非今者族]." He had also boasted that the Chinese Communist Party had executed a hundred times as many counter-revolutionary intellectuals as

---

[29] *Selected Works*, IV, p. 378. (*Analects* V, 14; Legge, p. 178.)
[30] *Mao Tse-tung Unrehearsed*, p. 82. (*Mencius*, VI, ii, 34; D. C. Lau, p. 201.)
[31] *Wan-sui* (1967), p. 48.
[32] *Mao Tse-tung Unrehearsed*, p. 208.
[33] *Ibid.*, p. 215.

Qin Shihuang, who had buried "only 460 Confucian scholars."[34]

But although Mao did not hesitate to invoke Qin Shihuang as a precursor, this does not mean that he took the same view of the historical significance of the Qin unification of the empire as did the ideologists of 1973-1975. At that time, Chairman Mao was said to have expounded, in his speech of 1958 just quoted, "the progressive role of revolutionary violence, and exposed the reactionary essence of attacks on Qin Shihuang as attacks on revolutionary violence and the dictatorship of the proletariat."[35] The conclusion, which is never stated outright, but is clearly implicit in materials of the mid-1970s, is that the Qin Shihuang analogy should, as it were, be turned inside out. Lin Biao had criticized Mao as a despot; right-minded people should, on the contrary, see Qin Shihuang as a revolutionary leader and the Qin autocracy as a kind of proto-proletarian dictatorship.

The analogy obviously requires that there should have been a change in the "mode of production," i.e., in the ruling class, and not merely a change in the organization of the state, with the founding of the Qin dynasty. The transition from slave-holding society to feudalism, which Mao himself had earlier placed, as we saw yesterday, in the eleventh century B.C., was therefore brought forward to the fifth, or even to the third century B.C. Conceivably, Mao might have changed his mind on this point since 1939, and in any case the views put forward in 1972-1974 had long been held by some Chinese historians. It is quite another matter to suggest, however, even if there *was* a change in the ruling class at the end of the third century B.C., that the "new rising landlord class" was consciously re-shaping Chinese society, taking Legalist ideology as its guide, in the same sense that the Communists, armed with Marxism-Leninism-Mao-Zedong Thought, are doing so today. Such a view was totally un-Marxist, and historically absurd, and there is no evidence that Mao ever espoused it—though there is no proof that he did not, either. The only rationale for this line of argument (apart from justifying the role öf the "Legalist leading group around the emperor" in its modern metamorphosis) would appear to reside in a desire to demonstrate that China had revolutionary power, and revolutionary ideology, before anyone else. Mao's position, even in his later years, was less crude, and despite his pride in China's cultural heritage, less narrowly nationalistic.

In the domain of modernization and economic development, after the upheaval of 1966-1969, and the further disruption caused by the struggle against Lin Biao, a new compromise appeared to be emerging in 1971-1972.

[34] *Wan-sui* (1969), p. 195.

[35] Jin Zhibai 靳志柏, "Pi-Kong yu luxian douzheng" 批孔與路線鬥爭 (Criticism of Confucius and Two-Line Struggle), *Hongqi*, no. 7, 1974, p. 32; *Peking Review*, no. 33, 1974, p. 11 and note 2.

This second and revised version of what might be called "mainstream Maoism" was in many respects similar to the ideas promoted, or accepted by Mao in the early 1960s. It called for preserving, in more moderate form, the anti-elitist and participatory thrust of the Cultural Revolution, while reviving the emphasis on technical progress and rapid economic growth which had always been an integral part of Mao's thought. And yet, even before the death of Zhou Enlai, who had been the architect of this policy, the compromise had been overturned. All recognition of the importance of professional skills had been swallowed up in an orgy of political rhetoric, and all things foreign were regarded as counter-revolutionary.

Much of the blame for the fact that the still-fragile equilibrium of 1972 was so soon shattered must no doubt be attributed to Mao's inability, old and ill as he was, to control the actions of his wife and her associates. But he had himself opened the door to these levelling and obscurantist excesses. Moreover, even though the stress on self-reliance to the point of isolation and xenophobia which emerged in 1973-1976 cannot be regarded as characteristic of Mao's own attitude, he did become increasingly sceptical in his last years, not so much about foreign knowledge as about specialized knowledge in general.

Without carrying his distrust of intellectuals to the point of characterizing them like the gang of four, as the "stinking ninth category," Mao therefore moved toward educational policies infinitely more extreme than those of the Great Leap Forward. "We shouldn't read too many books," he said in February 1964. "We should read Marxist books, but not too many of them either. It will be enough to read a dozen or so. If we read too many we can move toward our opposite, become bookworms, dogmatists, revisionists."[36]

Very soon, in the Cultural Revolution, Mao allowed the emergence of a situation in which few books indeed would be read by anyone, for a period of several years. To be sure, the evidence shows that he did not intend the disruption of academic work at last as long as this, but as in the case of the disorder created by the onslaught on the existing system as a whole, Mao cannot escape responsibility for the consequences of his acts. "We must smash and eliminate superstition," he had declared in January 1965, "we must not smash and eliminate science."[37] Beginning in 1966, however, Mao exalted the creativity of the masses, and ridiculed those who attached importance to specialized knowledge acquired through study, to a degree quite incompatible with his own insistence on the importance of science. In effect, he implemented to the letter the bitter joke current in China today: "*Wenhua geming shi ge wenhua de ming* 文化革命是革文化的命" (The Cultural Revolution was

[36] *Mao Tse-tung Unrehearsed*, p. 210.
[37] *Wan-sui* (1969), p. 605.

about doing away with culture).

But it was, in the last analysis, Mao's conception of the political process, and the way in which he exercised political power, which decisively shaped the heritage he left behind at his death. Throughout the decade from 1966 to 1976, Mao strove to combine in some fashion the strong leadership in which he continued to believe with the encouragement of initiative, and even of rebellion from below which had constituted the essential innovation of the Cultural Revolution. In one of the very last directives published in his lifetime, Mao was quoted in May 1976 as saying that revolutions would continue to break out in future because "junior officials, students, workers, peasants and soldiers do not like big shots oppressing them."[38] There is no way of verifying the authenticity of this text, which was published in the context of the campaign against Deng Xiaoping, but it sounds very much like the irrepressible Mao. Although he remained committed to the need for "heads," he could not resist the temptation to challenge them, and shake them up. Over this enterprise there continued to hang, however, a fundamental ambiguity, resulting from the fact that the right of the masses to "rebel" was guaranteed only by a figure exercising personal authority of a kind which was officially likened in China to that of the first Qin emperor. Moreover, in the late 1960s, the concept of *zhong* 忠 or loyalty to the ruler was introduced as perhaps the dominant political value in China at that time.

I do not believe that we should confuse Mao's view of these matters with that of Jiang Qing and the gang of four, who promoted an ideal of ceaseless contestation of all constituted authority, leading to a state of anarchy tempered and exploited by the rule of a palace clique. The fact remains, however, that it was he who had laid the foundations for these traditionalist deviations, and in no small measure encouraged them.

Thus far, in discussing the Cultural Revolution period, I have stressed primarily, as I have done throughout these lectures, Mao Zedong's ideas rather than the uses to which they were put. In the case of the Cultural Revolution, however, it is even less possible than in dealing with the Chinese revolution as a whole to separate theory and policy from their concrete expression. For the dramatic and bloody events of Mao's last decade are graven into the minds of the Chinese people, and necessarily affect profoundly not only their view of his policies during the years 1966-1976, but their overall estimation of the man and his work.

In 1968, I wrote of the Cultural Revolution:

> In launching this movement, Mao was actuated by motives both noble and base.
> I do not scruple to use these very strong words, though the first will cause

---

[38] *Renmin ribao*, 16 May, 1976; translated in *Peking Review*, no. 21, 1976, p. 9.

indignation in some, and the second in others. It is truly noble to pursue an aim which, in its ultimate dimension, is nothing less than the creation of a new humanity no longer corrupted by the instincts of greed and domination. It is truly base not merely to cast aside but to accuse of the most monstrous crimes one's comrades of forty years' standing, without whose collective support victory in the revolution could never have been won, to assume all their merits for oneself, and to encourage and glory in a cult of one's own infallibility and supernatural virtue which makes Stalin look like a modest man.[39]

Judgments such as this, and the fact that I had referred, in a passage added to my biography of Mao Zedong in January 1967, to large numbers of people beaten to death by the Red Guards, led me to be denounced at the time as an "anti-Chinese element." Now the evaluation just quoted would probably be regarded by many Chinese as if anything too indulgent.

The blackest aspect of Mao's behaviour was undoubtedly his propensity to wreak vengeance on those who had slighted or crossed him. I noted earlier Mao's endorsement of the maxim: "*Yi gu fei jin zhe zu.*" In the Cultural Revolution, precisely this principle was implemented. The "Three-Family Village" of Deng Tuo 鄧拓 , Wu Han 吳晗 , and Liao Mosha 廖沫沙, had, as you all know, criticized Mao in veiled historical analogies in the early 1960s. The first of these was hounded to suicide on 16 and 17 May, 1966, at the very moment when Mao took personal charge of the Cultural Revolution. As for Wu Han, not only was he driven to death himself; his wife and all but one of his children also perished, though that may not have been the result of a conscious decision from above.

Of the tens of thousands of violent deaths which occurred during the years 1966-1976, very many must unquestionably be put down to the political ambitions and personal spite of Jiang Qing and her allies, and may have taken place with only Mao's passive acquiescence, or even without his knowledge. I am thinking, for example, of the truly harrowing tale of Zhang Zhixin 張志新 , the critic of Cultural Revolution orthodoxy in 1970-1975, whose vocal cords were removed before she was shot on 4 April, 1975 to prevent her from crying out, or of the fate of writers such as Lao She 老舍 , and intellectuals such as Li Da. Nor did Mao, like Stalin, revel in blood for blood's sake. But some deaths, such as those of Deng Tuo and Wu Han, or his erstwhile successor Liu Shaoqi, persecuted to death in December 1969, must be blamed primarily on Mao himself. Even if he did not explicitly order that they be killed, a word from him would have saved them—and he chose not to utter that word. In this respect, he was indeed a faithful successor to Qin Shihuang.

As for the positive motive I attributed to Mao in 1968, namely the

[39] S. Schram, "Social Revolution and Cultural Revolution in China," in B. Towers (ed.), *China and the West: Mankind Evolving* (London: Garnstone Press, 1970), p. 74.

creation of a new socialist man, the fashionable orthodoxy of that time has now been stood on its head. Then, the apostles of the "New Left" in Europe and America imagined that a paradise after their own hearts had emerged in the East. "I have seen the future, and it works," said one colleague (who shall be nameless) on returning from his first visit to China around 1970. Today, many of these same "New Leftists" are outraged to discover that China has not after all dispensed entirely with things such as authority, status, and constraint, and dismiss the entire Chinese experience, both political and economic, as simply a thinly-disguised variant of the Stalinist model. A corollary of this judgment is that Mao himself was a cynical dictator concerned with nothing save his own power, and utterly uninterested in human values of any description.

It should be apparent from my discussion of Mao's thinking in the 1950s that I do not believe his vision of a socialist society can be regarded as nothing but an ideological fig-leaf. On the other hand, it is quite certain that, in Mao's last years, personal considerations came increasingly to take precedence over broader goals. Moreover, even to the extent that he did still seek to pursue China's welfare rather than simply his own, he did so in such extreme and unbalanced ways that what I called, in 1968, his "noble" motives were substantially defeated by the methods he chose.

No doubt this was partly because Mao allowed himself to be carried away by his own enthusiasm, and partly because he relied on his own capacity to shift the emphasis to the opposite pole of one of the contradictions inherent in his policies whenever the development of the situation required it. The result was, however, that in practice "Maoism" came to mean more and more, both in China and outside it, reliance on political zeal as a substitute for, rather than a spur to, the effective mobilization of economic and technical resources for development, and above all a policy of relentlessly levelling down rather than up, in everything from education to material rewards.

It was precisely this caricature of Mao's ideas of the 1950s and early 1960s (a caricature for which he himself was largely responsible) which had such wide appeal a decade ago, and is still fiercely defended in some quarters. The Chinese, who have seen such Maoism in action, for the most part want none of it, and dismiss it under the two headings of "voluntarism" and "egalitarianism." The experience of Mao's last decade, during which the population was constantly mobilized by contending groups in the leadership for conflicting aims, manipulated, used, their work disrupted and their personal lives shattered, has inevitably left its mark. It would, however, in my opinion, be wrong to assume that because of the destruction wrought by an old man clinging desperately to life and power, the Chinese people have repudiated, or will necessarily repudiate the whole of the Maoist heritage.

Let me now in conclusion try to sum up briefly my view, first as to whether the current Chinese leadership is bent on consigning Mao's heritage to oblivion, and then as to how history may remember him.

The first of these questions should be re-phrased. It is quite plain that there is no intention whatsoever in Beijing of launching a process of "de-Maoization," or even of discrediting the body of doctrine known as Mao Zedong Thought. The problem is rather what they mean by this latter term, and whether behind the label there remains anything of the substance. The essence of the current approach is to use "Mao Zedong Thought" to designate not only Mao's own positive contributions to the application of Marxism in China, but good and useful works by Liu Shaoqi, Zhou Enlai, and others, provided these deal with themes which Mao Zedong himself at least evoked or sketched out, and not with aspects of Marxism completely absent from his own works. As far as Mao himself is concerned, a clear distinction is, of course, drawn between his positive contributions and the "errors' of his later years." The former (chiefly dating from the period 1927-1957) still provide the main corpus of Mao Zedong Thought. Mao's writings of later years, in which he is said to have violated his own principles, are on the contrary excluded from the authentic collection of ideas and theories bearing his name.

In effect, what they are trying to do is to rescue Mao Zedong from himself. Are they in fact saving him, or mutilating him? For my part, I would be tempted to say that they are carrying out a surgical operation—an operation which aims to save the life, or rather the reputation, of the patient, but a surgical operation none the less.

Let me explain. The question was frequently debated, from 1966 onwards, whether the Cultural Revolution constituted the natural outgrowth and culmination of Mao's previous ideas and actions. Some people, especially at the outset, were inclined to dismiss it as merely a senile aberration. Others, including of course those in the West who sought inspiration and guidance from Mao and his thought, saw the policies inaugurated in 1966 not only as the culmination and supreme achievement of Mao's career, but as the goal toward which all his previous activity had been tending.

I have never accepted either of these views. On more than one aspect of Mao's career I have changed my interpretation over the years (hence this present attempt as a reassessment), but on this point, my view has been exactly the same since 1966. I see the Cultural Revolution not as *the* necessary and ineluctable culmination of Mao's approach to revolution, but as *one* possible, and entirely logical outcome of his life. In other words, he was not fated to end like this, but neither is it surprising that he did.

It is perfectly true that, as the Chinese say today, Mao in his later years violated in many respects his own principles. For example, from the time of the Great Leap Forward, he abandoned the attitude of realism, and of carrying out investigations and experiments before launching major new policies which he had always preached, and on the whole observed, prior to 1958. But if the maxim "seeking the truth from facts" had long been an integral part of Mao's outlook, the impulses which led to its abandonment or distortion were also present before 1958. As we have seen, he expressed as early as 1928 his faith in the mighty power of subjective forces.

Thus, to reiterate, while Mao need not necessarily have committed the errors of his last years, neither can they be dismissed as simply the accidental vagaries of an old man. They can plausibly be seen as organically linked to his thought, even though many people today, both in China and outside, regard them as unwholesome excrescences rather than part of the sound body of his doctrine. Indeed, Mao himself may well have believed to the end that the Cultural Revolution was his crowning achievement—though this does not, of course, oblige us to accept his own subjective judgment. Such being the case, to excise whole periods from the record of Mao's work and Thought must, I think, be regarded as a surgical operation.

From the standpoint of the current Chinese leadership, such an operation is an entirely rational proceeding, and I think that, in the short term at least, the prospects are very good that it will succeed. Certainly, those ideas which have been rejected, and excluded from Mao Zedong Thought as now defined, have little appeal to the great majority of cadres and intellectuals in the cities. What I do not know, as a foreign observer, is how much residual attachment to the Maoism of the Cultural Revolution there may be in the countryside— where I have spent relatively little time—and in the PLA—with which I have had no contacts at all. Even if there is more than I think, I do not believe this will cause serious problems threatening the unity and stability of China so long as the present policies are seen to work.

The real problem seems to me to reside not so much in the surgical operation to remove the errors of Mao's later years, as in the limited substance, and above all in the limited number of ideas useful as a guide to China's future development, in what is left of Mao Zedong Thought after the operation.

Few would deny Mao Zedong the major share of the credit for devising the pattern of struggle based on guerrilla warfare in the countryside which ultimately led to victory in the civil war. Most Chinese are undoubtedly grateful to him for his achievements in overthrowing the corrupt and oppressive regime of the Guomindang, giving the land to the peasants, and restoring China's independence and sovereignty, and these achievements must be taken into account in any attempt to assess his historical role. The struggle for liberation belongs, however, to the past, and while it may supply material for heroic legends, cannot itself provide direct guidance for current policies—as the disastrous consequences of the attempt to revive aspects of the "Yan'an model" during and after the Great Leap have abundantly demonstrated. As for those aspects of Mao's heritage which are stressed today as the core of his Thought—basing policies on investigation of the facts, a role (not always clearly defined) for the people in running their own affairs, symbolized by the "mass line," the principle of self-reliance in foreign affairs—they almost certainly command general support, but they do not in themselves add up to a revolutionary theory of a distinctive stamp. It could be said that they are almost as abstract as the "standpoint, viewpoint and method" which Mao Zedong proposed in 1938 to take over from Marx. Either these principles constitute simply a set of supplementary hypotheses, and the ideological foundation of the Chinese People's Republic is to consist henceforth in Marxism, or Marxism-Leninism; or a whole new set of theories has still in large part to be elaborated, taking the contributions of Mao and others of his generation as a starting-point, and Mao's name as a label, or a banner, but breaking new ground in many respects.

In my opinion, it is the latter course which those with most influence in the Chinese Communist Party intend to follow. But before I consider the prospects for the success of this enterprise, it is time I offered you the reassessment of Mao Zedong and his Thought promised in the title of these lectures. I cannot presume to speak either for history, or for the Chinese people. My conclusions therefore have no claim to be authoritative, or definitive. That being said, here are a few ideas for discussion.

As I indicated in reply to a question from a journalist at the press conference last week, I agree with the current Chinese view that Mao's merits outweighed his faults, but it is not easy to put a figure on the positive and negative aspects. How does one weigh, for example, the good fortune of hundreds of millions of peasants in getting land against the execution, in the course of land reform and the "Campaign against Counter-Revolutionaries," or in other contexts, of millions, some of whom certainly deserved to die, but others of whom undoubtedly did not? How does one balance the achievements in economic development during the first Five-Year Plan, or during the whole twenty-seven years of Mao's leadership after 1949, against the starvation which came in the wake of the misguided enthusiasm of the Great Leap Forward, or the bloody shambles of the Cultural Revolution? One can, of course, make an approximate calculation on the basis of the number of years when Mao's line was, generally speaking, correct, and the number of years when it was not. Taking the official Chinese assessment according to which Mao was right most of the time before 1949, and somewhat less than half the time after 1949, this would lead to something like the *san-qi pingjia* 三七評價 of Mao's own assessment of Stalin. But this is hardly a scientific basis for

judging the proportions either, for one year of outstanding success, or of disastrous failure, may weigh heavier in the balance than several indifferent years.

In any case, a precise quantitative judgment, or even an absolutely firm
and categorical judgment as to whether Mao did more good or more bad in
the course of his life as a whole, is really important only to the Chinese, and
to those in other revolutionary movements throughout the world who look,
or have looked, to China for leadership. They must formulate such a judgment, because they must decide whether they wish to accept his political
legacy, in some form at least, or whether they choose to reject it.

For an outside observer such as myself, this question is less important than
determining which aspects of Mao's Thought still have some positive significance, and which represent errors to be avoided. I trust you will agree that I
have not shrunk back, in these lectures, from bestowing both praise and
blame. In the last analysis, however, I am more interested in the potential
future impact of his thought than in sending Mao as an individual to Heaven
or to Hell.

In assessing particular aspects of Mao's Thought, I propose to look now at
four points, all of which, as we have seen, have a history extending back
beyond 1949: the relation between China and foreign countries; the role of
human and subjective factors in the revolutionary process; the relation
between democracy and centralism; and the analysis of contradictions in
Chinese society.

The problem of the relation between China and foreign countries falls into
two parts. On the one hand, there is the matter of China's independence and
autonomy, vis-à-vis both the Soviets and the other old-fashioned imperialists.
This is something on which Mao insisted, to the extent circumstances per-
mitted, from the time he took de facto control of the Chinese Communist
Party in 1935, and which he stressed, and implemented, even more firmly in
his later years. On the whole, virtually everyone (except the Soviets) regards
this as a positive achievement, and so do I. On the other hand, there is the
question of the interaction between Chinese culture and ideas of Western
origin, Marxism in particular. Here, in my view, Mao was notably less successful. He was right to seek to preserve China's own identity, but in the end his
attempt to combine Chinese and Western ideas produced not a synthesis, but
an uneasy amalgam, symbolized by the juxtaposition in 1975 of two campaigns taking their inspiration from Qin Shihuang on the one hand, and
Marx and his disciples on the other. It could no doubt scarcely be otherwise
with a man of Mao's generation, who was not really exposed to foreign
influences until he was already an adult. The consequence is, however, that
the whole problem of encountering the reality of Western society and culture,
assessing the utility or otherwise of various ideas for China, and forging a true

synthesis, must be approached almost from scratch. That process has been underway in earnest for the last four years. It would have produced less of a "culture shock" in China, with all the attendant risks of social instability, if Mao had made more of a start in his lifetime.

As regards the role of human and subjective factors, I have made it clear that in my view, Mao went much too far, from the late 1920s onwards, in asserting their omnipotence. On the other hand, I wonder whether the present Chinese leaders are not still so acutely conscious of the disastrous consequences of the Great Leap attempt to carry out, through the mobilization of human energies, changes in the economy and in patterns of social organization for which the objective conditions were simply not ripe, and of the Cultural Revolution attempt to "touch people to their very souls," which tore apart the fabric of human relations, that they distrust any reference to this dimension of the revolutionary process. Personally, I think that in future it may prove possible to rehabilitate something of Mao Zedong's emphasis on man, and on the superstructure, without succumbing to the orgies of voluntarism into which Mao led China on more than one occasion.

The issue of democracy and centralism, and of the meaning of the "mass line," immediately raises the question of the nature and limits of the "high-level democracy" to which the present Chinese leadership aspires. I shall say a few words about that in a moment, by way of conclusion (for I think it is *the* great question at the present time). Here I merely note that, as I have already suggested repeatedly in various contexts, I do not think Mao Zedong left his successors with a very sound basis on which to build. He left them, certainly, with something, namely with the insight, which is an integral part of the doctrine of the "mass line," that ordinary people, and lower-level authorities, should be involved in their own affairs. His discussions of these issues, however, were always set either in the context of a Leninist, or Stalinist, Party dictatorship, or in that of an old-fashioned Chinese despotism or autocracy. In his last interview with Edgar Snow, in December 1970, Mao indicated that, at the present stage, the Chinese people could not do without an emperor figure to worship.[40] I believe he was wrong, and/or that they have subsequently awakened. In any case, his notion of participation was a strange hybrid, and an authentic form of socialist democracy in China has still to be invented, and implemented.

Finally, I believe that there is also a tendency in China today to be perhaps unduly wary of Mao's vision of the world, and of Chinese society in particular, in terms of the omnipresence of contradictions. As I have argued at greater length in the article I published last year in *The China Quarterly* regarding the

[40]Edgar Snow, *The Long Revolution* (London: Hutchison, 1972).

first sixty years of the Chinese Communist Party, this is natural enough, given the consequences of Mao's glorification of contradictions and disequilibrium in the economic sphere at the time of the Great Leap, and the appalling human cost of his Cultural Revolution utopia of class struggle.[41] But, kept within proper bounds, Mao's lively sense of the tension and contradictions existing in a modernizing society (and indeed in every society) may perhaps have a positive role to play.

I said I would conclude with a few words about the current situation. Plainly, the current reforming leadership is walking a tightrope. I remain convinced that there is under way a serious attempt to create new forms of "high-level democracy." At the same time, all leading cadres, however unorthodox their views, are committed to the maintenance of ultimate Party control. Any attempts at "democratization" (a term widely used in China a year or two ago, but less common today) must therefore somehow be pursued without falling off the tightrope either into an old-fashioned Leninist Party state, or into Polish-style confrontation.

Such an enterprise may well appear like squaring the circle. Certainly, the experience thus far indicates it will be very difficult to break out of the old Maoist approach to the "mass line," with its overriding emphasis on centralism. Over the past two years, inputs from below have repeatedly been solicited (as in the matter of local elections), but as soon as these have materialized the leadership (or some elements in the leadership) has taken fright, and has intervened to crush, or in any case to curtail these initiatives. At the same time, it is all too easy to ridicule and dismiss, from Hong Kong, or from Europe or America, these first tentative steps toward reform, without taking account of the many problems which have to be overcome.

There is, first of all, the weight of two great traditions of bureaucratic rule, Soviet and Chinese, both of which, despite the episode of the Cultural Revolution, are an integral part of the heritage which Mao handed over to his successors. The first defines the Party's role in such a way that it does not merely provide guidance and general orientation, but effectively exercises substantive control at all levels. The second inculcates in officials a profound suspicion of any activity, from forming associations to digging up the bowels of the earth, which is not under the firm control of the authorities. And there are, of course, many people strongly marked by both these traditions in China, who will be quick to take advantage of any hint of disorder. Moreover, Mao's legacy of rebellion, as well as his legacy of authoritarianism, has created tensions within Chinese society which make a responsible and measured

---

[41] S. Schram, "To Utopia and Back: a Cycle in the History of the Chinese Communist Party," *The China Quarterly*, no. 87 (September 1981), especially pp. 433-439.

response to reform less likely.

Moreover, the limited and sketchy character of those elements of Mao Zedong's contribution still regarded as correct and acceptable creates a situation in which, if new ideas cannot be elaborated fast enough to fill the gaps, there is a strong and very natural temptation simply to fall back on orthodox Leninism as a solution to any pressing problem. This is, in effect, what has happened with the obsessive emphasis on Party leadership, as a response to the obstreperousness of young people, many of whom are not so much "dissidents" as simply non-conformists. The axiom of ultimate Party control is, as I have already noted, a point on which the Chinese authorities cannot possibly compromise; but the heavy-handed insistence on this principle to some extent echoes the Soviet response to similar problems. And, as I have said in last year's *China Quarterly* article, I regard the Soviet model not so much as a utopia as a dead end.

There is also the possibility, if no response can be found in the new version of Mao Zedong Thought, to fall back on aspects of the "Old Testament" which appear, to outside observers at least, as singularly out of harmony with the current reforming policies taken as a whole. This is the case, for example, of the revival, as a solution to the "crisis of faith" which is said not to exist, but obviously does exist, among young people in China, of that decidedly shop-worn symbol Lei Feng 雷鋒. To be sure, Lei Feng does stand for devotion to the people, rather than one's own interests, and is therefore a logical counter to the rampant attachment to personal gain which appears to have emerged as a result of current economic policies, and exposure to Western "bourgeois" influences. But he also stands for "boundless fidelity to Chairman Mao," and in general for the whole rote-learning approach to political participation which Lin Biao ironically baptized "the living study and application of Mao Zedong Thought." This hardly seems compatible with the "liberation of thought" recently proclaimed as a goal in China.

Nevertheless, on balance I remain optimistic. If the present reforming policies in the political, economic, and cultural domains can be successfully applied for ten or twenty years, we may well see the emergence of a China which is truly a part of the modern world, while maintaining its own ideological autonomy and cultural identity, and where the name of Mao Zedong is still respected, and his ideas still play a role, as an element in a new synthesis, which must necessarily go beyond anything Mao himself could have imagined. That is, in my opinion, the only form in which Mao Zedong Thought can survive in China. For if the "whateverist" faction were ever to seize control, and seek to implement once more the failed policies of the Great Leap and/or of the Cultural Revolution decade, such an attempt could not last long, and at the next swing of the pendulum, or dialectical reversal, Mao Zedong Thought would probably have been discredited even as a label for policies substantially different from his.

Questions and Answers

Q. In one of your books you mentioned that you were very reluctant to use the term "Maoism." And I appreciate that. Now after the current leadership's "surgical operation," how do you think Maoism or Mao Zedong Thought as described in your book will survive?

A. There are two parts to your question. Why have I been using the term "Maoism" today, and secondly, will this thing, however you describe it, survive? Now, on the first point I still adhere to the opinion expressed in *The Political Thought of Mao Tse-tung* that it is better not to use the term "Maoism" to designate Mao's thought. I have used it, loosely, in these lectures, because it is shorter and more convenient than saying "the general complex of attitudes and policies associated with Mao Zedong" or something like that. But the total corpus of his thought must be called either Mao Zedong Thought, as the Chinese call it, or something similar. I would prefer not to call it "Maoism" because I don't think, apart from the fact that the Chinese don't use this terminology, that it is systematic enough to constitute a proper "ism." There is not a system of thought even to the extent that it appeared to be relatively systematic at one point; as I suggested in this lecture, the polarities unravelled and the syntheses broke down. I used "Maoism" loosely, and simply to suggest an association with Mao's approach to certain problems, but I would not use it to identify his thought.

   As to the second part of your question, namely whether I think Mao's thought as defined in that book will survive, I think some of it will survive, and some of it will not. The aspects of his thought likely to survive are some of those that the leadership in Beijing apparently wants to preserve. There are some things they esteem which I do not esteem quite so much, and there are several points, suggested in my conclusion, where they are perhaps so traumatized by the Cultural Revolution that they find it very hard to be detached. It is all very well for me, a foreigner who lives far away, as I said in my first lecture, to say "Perhaps you shouldn't go to extremes and throw out the baby with the bath-water." It is very hard to adopt this attitude if you have been in prison, or sent to the countryside to *zuo niupeng* 坐牛棚, or if like so many intellectuals you had a relative, friend, or a teacher beaten to death. None the less, I think that more of the dialectical character of Mao's thought, and the concern with the human dimension of politics may be reinstituted in less destructive forms.

Q. Will the critical evaluation of Mao currently underway remove impedi-
    ments to improving relations with the Soviet Union?
A. I am not an authority on foreign policy, but relying on general im-
    pressions I think that Mao's personal relationship with Khrushchev was
    not a good one. They rubbed one another the wrong way almost from
    the outset. Khrushchev did not treat Mao with the respect that he thought
    was due to a leader who had been around for a long time, and at the top
    for a longer period than himself. This personal factor was a very im-
    portant factor in bad relations. But there are several respects in which the
    reticence and even hostility between the Soviet Union and the Chinese
    goes much beyond personalities. There are undoubtedly questions of
    national interest. I am not about to suggest that the Chinese are ready to
    expand into Siberia. But there is the cultural and historical dimension.
    There are recollections of the events of the 1950s and 1960s when the
    Soviets regarded themselves as the big brother and were trying to tell the
    Chinese how to run things. I think that the Chinese continue to resent
    that. I can well imagine a moderate improvement in state-to-state
    relations. But any kind of intimate embrace would automatically make
    the Chinese junior partners, and I think there is no possibility at all that
    the Chinese would ever accept such a role.

    The Chinese utterly reject Brezhnev's doctrine of limited sovereignty,
    as proclaimed after the invasion of Czechoslovakia in 1968.

    So, Mao and Khrushchev did not get on together. Both men are gone.
    Brezhnev has not succeeded in ending the quarrel. He will be gone soon,
    but I think it unlikely that there will be an immediate reconciliation.

Q. The current Chinese leadership seems to want to separate Mao Zedong
    Thought and Mao's person. Do you see much merit in this treatment of
    Mao Zedong Thought? Is this a means on their part to escape from Mao's
    policies?
A. Before the redefinition in the June 1981 Resolution, there were already
    two definitions, if you like, of Mao Zedong Thought: (1) what he actually
    thought about, wrote and said during his long life, and (2) what was
    printed in the four volumes of his *Selected Works*, what was printed in
    his Red Book, and what was propagated in the 1960s and 1970s. Now we
    have a third definition of Mao Zedong Thought, which is, in effect,
    Marxism as it is correctly applied to China.* The Chinese still say that
    Mao made far and away a greater contribution himself than everyone else
    put together. His works are still regarded as good and correct, despite the
    errors of his later years. Zhou Enlai and others made contributions, but

*See the Preface.

Mao is still the major contributor to Mao Zedong Thought. It is the collective creation of the Chinese people through the leading figures of their Chinese Communist Party. I don't really see anything wrong with the way they are using the term. If they were to say that Mao Zedong Thought is what *Mao* thought, and in fact include a large amount of material written by Liu Shaoqi, that would be dishonest, and would lead to confusion. But if they say that Mao Zedong Thought is Marxism as expounded and implemented in China I see nothing unacceptable about this.

I do have to answer or try to answer your second question, which is, is this a halfway house, a stage toward getting rid of Mao completely. In other words, they use Mao Zedong Thought as a term meaning Marxism as it is correctly applied in China, with two-thirds Mao and one-third everybody else. Later they gradually weed out Mao's share until there is nothing left of him. I doubt very much that this can happen. It is possible to throw out someone who represents a phase in the development of the Communist Party. For example, at one time it seemed possible for Khrushchev to throw out Stalin, though when you look at the Soviet Union over the last 10 or 15 years, you wonder whether he is gone or still there. But to use my metaphor of a surgical operation, it is only if you have a strong trunk that you can grow a graft. If there is a strong Leninist trunk, then you can knock off a Stalinist branch. But if you knock off Mao, there is virtually nothing left. Mao is the trunk for China. Mao's heritage is being severely winnowed through, but some substantial part of Mao's writings and ideas will remain as the content of this label Mao Zedong Thought for a long time. However great the bitterness and resentment to which I alluded a moment ago, they can't say "Let's throw out everything and begin anew, discarding everything from the Chinese revolution for the last 50 years."

Q. Last year Solzhenitsyn wrote an article in the journal, *Foreign Affairs*. He was levelling an attack on Lenin in his attack on traditional Russian culture. Solzhenitsyn said something like "Stalin and Lenin had destroyed traditional Russian culture to the extent that the national recovery would take between fifty to two hundred years." Does it make sense to you to talk of the damage that Mao and the Cultural Revolution have done to China in those terms?

A. To my mind, no. With reference to China, I think that the damage caused by the errors of Mao's last years was limited by the basis which was constructed up to 1957. In the early 1960s when relatively sound and rational policies were implemented, China's foundation was a great deal sounder than that Stalin left behind. Secondly, I don't want to appear racist or culturalist, but in my view, on the whole, the stability and soundness of Chinese culture and society is greater than that of Russian culture and society. They have a tradition on which to build, a foundation which is more stable and solid than the one on which Lenin and Stalin built. So harm was certainly done, but economic and other indicators certainly show that China is moving forward, perhaps not as fast as the Chinese would like it to be but certainly faster than some countries. I think that the foundation is sound and do not think a century or century-and-a-half will be needed for recovery. The ambition of Mao and of his successors to catch up with the West and to become a truly modern country, with a level of production equivalent at least to that of the United States today, fifty years hence is another matter. Perhaps they will succeed, I hope for their sakes that they will succeed. I do not see Chinese society today as being in a shambles as a result of the Cultural Revolution, which happened mainly in the cities. The Great Leap Forward was a disaster which happened mainly in the countryside, but a reasonable degree of sanity was restored from the years of the early 1960s onwards. While policies were not ideal, they were reasonably sound. The bloodbath of the Cultural Revolution occurred mainly in the cities. But the cities are not simply, as some have suggested, peripheral phenomena or excrescences. The cities were an integral part of revolution as Mao conceived it. None the less, this event which shook the cities for a whole decade did not shatter the foundation of the whole of Chinese society. So I believe that there is a relatively sound basis.

Q. You have defined Mao Zedong Thought in three different ways. You have indicated that there really is no possible substitute for Mao since there is no Lenin, as in the Soviet Union. Mao Zedong Thought in the past twenty years has acquired the status of a national philosophy that Confucianism enjoyed in earlier times. How do you evaluate the place of Mao Zedong's Thought in the long sweep of Chinese history? Where does one put Confucianism and the *San min zhuyi* 三民主義 in this context?

A. I'm not sure that there is a big problem in deciding where to place Sun Yatsen's ideological heritage. He was a good guy, and contributed positively to the revolution but his body of thought never went deep in Chinese society. Confucianism is of course of quite a different order.

First of all, one must distinguish between the ideology of the leading party and the ideas present in society at large. As the Chinese themselves say, the Chinese Communist Party has "become a ruling party" (*bian cheng zhizhengdang* 變成執政黨), and this party which is firmly established as the ruling party, and which proposes to go on ruling China for the good of the Chinese people, and hopefully with the support and co-operation of the Chinese people, is going to have some kind of doctrine which will contain large elements drawn from Mao Zedong Thought. But that does not solve the problems of Chinese society and culture as a whole. However strong and authoritarian the Chinese Communist Party has been in its rule at some times, and particularly in Mao's last years, the Chinese system is not the kind of system in which every idea of every individual is dictated and shaped by a doctrine from on high. Most people, even the Chinese that I know, are not always thinking about politics. Most people's minds are not occupied with political doctrine. The whole fabric of Chinese culture and civilization is still there, and something has to be done through it or with it.

Basically, Mao's approach was that it was necessary to create a new modern Chinese culture which would incorporate all the valid elements from the old Chinese culture. It would have a version of Marxism-Leninism as its leading political ideology, but would be enriched by everything in the whole heritage of Chinese culture which was not regarded as pernicious and reactionary. Now, it is not easy to construct such a synthesis. In my opinion Mao himself did not really synthesize the Marxist ideas which were in his head and the Confucian and Taoist ideas which were also undoubtedly there. To reshape the thinking of the entire Chinese people, in accordance with such a synthesis, is of course an even longer-term and more complex operation. We are discussing a problem which the Chinese people confront existentially every day of their lives.

You as intellectuals and as students in Hong Kong are bicultural. Many of you genuinely participate in two cultures, as few people do. This problem of an existential synthesis, a concrete synthesis of historical and social development in two very different historical traditions is an enormous problem. The Chinese have not solved it yet. Mao might have done more than he did but it was difficult for him to do more than he did. He was extremely aware of its existence, and talked about this problem all the time. Confucius has not gone away; Confucius will not go away. The late Joseph Levenson, for whom I had great respect, had his "museum theory" of Chinese culture. He said that the Chinese communists had consigned Confucius and all the rest of their traditional culture to a museum where they could admire them from time to time and say, "Look what a high culture we Chinese had." It was there in their museum, and had no relevance to their lives. I don't believe that. Chinese culture had a very real and living meaning for Mao throughout his life. Exactly how Confucianism and Marxism will interact in China in the future is a problem for the Chinese people and their government to decide.

CONCLUDING REMARKS—Dr. Byron Weng

It remains for me to thank Professor Schram for the three lectures he has given us. For some years it has been said that the task of our era was to find a synthesis for capitalism and socialism. Professor Schram's lectures have inspired me to think that perhaps in our case, judging from what has been going on for the last few years under the leadership of Deng Xiaoping, we need to find some kind of synthesis between Confucianism and socialism as well. The three things, Confucianism, socialism and capitalism, must come together and become a workable body of ideas for handling China's problems. And I think that this will be a challenge for many, many years to come. These are complicated thoughts, and I am very glad that we have had the opportunity to learn from Professor Schram's lectures, which have provided many helpful ideas, as we search for answers in this general direction. May I again say, Thank you, Professor Schram, and thank you all for coming to these lectures.

Mao in Guangzhou, 1925.

Mao in Ruijin, Jiangxi Province, 1931.

Mao attending the Yan'an Forum on Literature and Art, May 1942.

Mao and Chou Enlai in Yan'an, 1937.

Mao and Chou Enlai at a meeting in 1953.

Mao presiding over the Second Session of the First National Committee of the Chinese People's Political Consultative Conference in 1950, which discussed and adopted the national emblem of the People's Republic of China.

Mao at work in his cave-dwelling in the Date Orchard, Yan'an, 1946.

Mao during the fighting in northern Shaanxi in 1947.

Mao revising the *Constitution of the People's Republic of China* (Draft), 1954.

Mao with Chou Enlai, Zhu De and Deng Xiaoping at the Second Session of the Eighth Party Congress, May 1958.

Mao receiving commanders and fighters of an air force unit of the PLA, 1964.

Mao chatting with commune members in Shaoshan, 1959.

Mao reviewing for the first time the Red Guards from Tian An Men Gate, 18 August, 1966.

Mao at the Tenth National Congress of the Communist Party of China, 1973.

Mao died in Beijing on 9 September, 1976.

On Questions of Party History

—Resolution on Certain Questions in the History of Our Party Since the Founding of the People's Republic of China

(Adopted by the Sixth Plenary Session of the 11th Central Committee
of the Communist Party of China on June 27, 1981)

Comrade Mao Zedong's Historical Role and Mao Zedong Thought

27. Comrade Mao Zedong was a great Marxist and a great proletarian revolutionary, strategist and theorist. It is true that he made gross mistakes during the "cultural revolution," but, if we judge his activities as a whole, his contributions to the Chinese revolution far outweigh his mistakes. His merits are primary and his errors secondary. He rendered indelible meritorious service in founding and building up our Party and the Chinese People's Liberation Army, in winning victory for the cause of liberation of the Chinese people, in founding the People's Republic of China and in advancing our socialist cause. He made major contributions to the liberation of the oppressed nations of the world and to the progress of mankind.

28. The Chinese Communists, with Comrade Mao Zedong as their chief representative, made a theoretical synthesis of China's unique experience in its protracted revolution in accordance with the basic principles of Marxism-Leninism. This synthesis constituted a scientific system of guidelines befitting China's conditions, and it is this synthesis which is Mao Zedong Thought, the product of the integration of the universal principles of Marxism-Leninism with the concrete practice of the Chinese revolution. Making revolution in a large Eastern semi-colonial, semi-feudal country is bound to meet with many special, complicated problems, which cannot be solved by reciting the general principles of Marxism-Leninism or by copying foreign experience in every detail. The erroneous tendency of making Marxism a dogma and deifying Comintern resolutions and the experience of the Soviet Union prevailed in the international communist movement and in our Party mainly in the late 1920s and early 1930s, and this tendency pushed the Chinese revolution to the brink of total failure. It was in the course of combating this wrong tendency and making a profound summary of our historical experience in this respect that Mao Zedong Thought took shape and developed. It was systematized and extended in a variety of fields and reached maturity in the

latter part of the Agrarian Revolutionary War and the War of Resistance Against Japan, and it was further developed during the War of Liberation and after the founding of the People's Republic of China. Mao Zedong Thought is Marxism-Leninsm applied and developed in China; it constitutes a correct theory, a body of correct principles and a summary of the experiences that have been confirmed in the practice of the Chinese revolution, a crystallization of the collective wisdom of the Chinese Communist Party. Many outstanding leaders of our Party made important contributions to the formation and development of Mao Zedong Thought, and they are synthesized in the scientific works of Comrade Mao Zedong.

29. Mao Zedong Thought is wide-ranging in content. It is an original theory which has enriched and developed Marxism-Leninism in the following respects:

1) On the new-democratic revolution. Proceeding from China's historical and social conditions, Comrade Mao Zedong made a profound study of the characteristics and laws of the Chinese revolution, applied and developed the Marxist-Leninist thesis of the leadership of the proletariat in the democratic revolution, and established the theory of new-democratic revolution—a revolution against imperialism, feudalism and bureaucrat-capitalism waged by the masses of the people on the basis of the worker-peasant alliance under the leadership of the proletariat. His main works on this subject include: *Analysis of the Classes in Chinese Society, Report on an Investigation of the Peasant Movement in Hunan, A Single Spark Can Start a Prairie Fire, Introducing "The Communist," On New Democracy, On Coalition Government* and *The Present Situation and Our Tasks.* The basic points of this theory are:

I) China's bourgeoisie consisted of two sections, the big bourgeoisie (that is, the comprador bourgeoisie, or the bureaucrat-bourgeoisie) which was dependent on imperialism, and the national burgeoisie which had revolutionary leanings but wavered. The proletariat should endeavour to get the national bourgeoisie to join in the united front under its leadership and in special circumstances to include even part of the big bourgeoisie in the united front, so as to isolate the main enemy to the greatest possible extent. When forming a united front with the bourgeoisie, the proletariat must preserve its own independence and pursue the policy of "unity, struggle, unity through struggle"; when forced to split with the bourgeoisie, chiefly the big bourgeoisie, it should have the courage and ability to wage a resolute armed struggle against the big bourgeoisie, while continuing to win the sympathy of the national bourgeoisie or keep it neutral.

II) Since there was no bourgeois democracy in China and the reactionary ruling classes enforced their terroristic dictatorship over the people by armed force, the revolution could not but essentially take the form of protracted armed struggle. China's armed struggle was a revolutionary war led by the proletariat with the peasants as the principal force. The peasantry was the most reliable ally of the proletariat. Through its vanguard, it was possible and necessary for the proletariat, with its progressive ideology and its sense of organization and discipline, to raise the political consciousness of the peasant masses, establish rural base areas, wage a protracted revolutionary war and build up and expand the revolutionary forces.

Comrade Mao Zedong pointed out that "the united front and armed struggle are the two basic weapons for defeating the enemy." Together with Party building, they constituted the "three magic weapons" of the revolution. They were the essential basis which enabled the Chinese Communist Party to become the core of leadership of the whole nation and to chart the course of encircling the cities from the countryside and finally winning countrywide victory.

2) On the socialist revolution and socialist construction. On the basis of the economic and political conditions for the transition to socialism ensuing on victory in the new-democratic revolution, Comrade Mao Zedong and the Chinese Communist Party followed the path of effecting socialist industrialization simultaneously with socialist transformation and adopted concrete policies for the gradual transformation of the private ownership of the means of production, thereby providing a theoretical as well as practical solution of the difficult task of building socialism in a large country such as China, a country which was economically and culturally backward, with a population accounting for nearly one-fourth of the world's total. By putting forward the thesis that the combination of democracy for the people and dictatorship over the reactionaries constitutes the people's democratic dictatorship, Comrade Mao Zedong enriched the Marxist-Leninist theory of the dictatorship of the proletarist. After the establishment of the socialist system, Comrade Mao Zedong pointed out that, under socialism, the people had the same fundamental interests, but that all kinds of contradictions still existed among them, and that contradictions between the enemy and the people and contradictions among the people should be strictly distinguished from each other and correctly handled. He proposed that among the people we should follow a set of correct policies. We should follow the policy of "unity—criticism—unity" in political matters, the policy of "long-term coexistence and mutual supervision" in the Party's relations with the democratic parties, the policy of "let a hundred flowers blossom, let a hundred schools of thought contend" in science and culture, and, in the economic sphere the

policy of overall arrangement with regard to the different strata in town and country and of consideration for the interests of the state, the collective and the individual, all three. He repeatedly stressed that we should not mechanically transplant the experience of foreign countries, but should find our own way to industrialization, a way suited to China's condition, by proceeding from the fact that China is a large agricultural country, taking agriculture as the foundation of the economy, correctly handling the relationship between heavy industry on the one hand and agriculture and light industry on the other and attaching due importance to the development of the latter. He stressed that in socialist construction we should properly handle the relationships between economic construction and building up defence, between large-scale enterprises and small and medium-scale enterprises, between the Han nationality and the minority nationalities, between the coastal regions and the interior, between the central and the local authorities, and between self-reliance and learning from foreign countries, and that we should properly handle the relationship between accumulation and consumption and pay attention to overall balance. Moreover, he stressed that the workers were the masters of their enterprises and that cadres must take part in physical labour and workers in management, that irrational rules and regulations must be reformed and that the three-in-one combination of technical personnel, workers and cadres must be effected. And he formulated the strategic idea of bringing all positive factors into play and turning negative factors into positive ones so as to unite the whole Chinese people and build a powerful socialist country. The important ideas of Comrade Mao Zedong concerning the socialist revolution and socialist construction are mainly contained in such major works as *Report to the Second Plenary Session of the Seventh Central Committee of the Communist Party of China, On the People's Democratic Dictatorship, On the Ten Major Relationships, On the Correct Handling of Contradictions Among the People* and *Talk at an Enlarged Work Conference Convened by the Central Committee of the Communist Party of China.*

3) On the building of the revolutionary army and military strategy. Comrade Mao Zedong methodically solved the problem of how to turn a revolutionary army chiefly made up of peasants into a new type of people's army which is proletarian in character, observes strict discipline and forms close ties with the masses. He laid it down that the sole purpose of the people's army is to serve the people wholeheartedly, he put forward the principle that the Party commands the gun and not the other way round, he advanced the Three Main Rules of Discipline and the Eight Points for Attention and stressed the practice of political, economic and military democracy and the principles of the unity of officers and soldiers, the unity

of army and people and the disintegration of the enemy forces, thus formulating by way of summation a set of policies and methods concerning political work in the army. In his military writings such as *On Correcting Mistaken Ideas in the Party, Problems of Strategy in China's Revolutionary War, Problems of Strategy in Guerrilla War Against Japan, On Protracted War* and *Problems of War and Strategy*, Comrade Mao Zedong summed up the experience of China's protracted revolutionary war and advanced the comprehensive concept of building a people's army and of building rural base areas and waging people's war by employing the people's army as the main force and relying on the masses. Raising guerrilla war to the strategic plane, he maintained that guerrilla warfare and mobile warfare of a guerrilla character would for a long time be the main forms of operation in China's revolutionary war. He explained that it would be necessary to effect an appropriate change in military strategy simultaneously with the changing balance of forces between the enemy and ourselves and with the progress of the war. He worked out a set of strategies and tactics for the revolutionary army to wage people's war in conditions when the enemy was strong and we were weak. These strategies and tactics include fighting a protracted war strategically and campaigns and battles of quick decision, turning strategic inferiority into superiority in campaigns and battles and concentrating a superior force to destroy the enemy forces one by one. During the War of Liberation, he formulated the celebrated 10 major principles of operation. All these ideas constitute Comrade Mao Zedong's outstanding contribution to the military theory of Marxism-Leninism. After the founding of the People's Republic, he put forward the important guideline that we must strengthen our national defence and build modern revolutionary armed forces (including the navy, the air force and technical branches) and develop modern defence technology (including the making of nuclear weapons for self-defence).

4) On policy and tactics. Comrade Mao Zedong penetratingly elucidated the vital importance of policy and tactics in revolutionary struggles. He pointed out that policy and tactics were the life of the Party, that they were both the starting-point and the end-result of all the practical activities of a revolutionary party and that the Party must formulate its policies in the light of the existing political situation, class relations, actual circumstances and the changes in them, combining principle and flexibility. He made many valuable suggestions concerning policy and tactics in the struggle against the enemy, in the united front and other questions. He pointed out among other things:

that, under changing subjective and objective conditions, a weak revolutionary force could ultimately defeat a strong reactionary force;

that we should despise the enemy strategically and take the enemy seriously tactically;

that we should keep our eyes on the main target of struggle and not hit out in all directions;

that we should differentiate between and disintegrate our enemies, and adopt the tactic of making use of contradictions, winning over the many, opposing the few and crushing our enemies one by one;

that, in areas under reactionary rule, we should combine legal and illegal struggle and, organizationally, adopt the policy of assigning picked cadres to work underground;

that, as for members of the defeated reactionary classes and reactionary elements, we should give them a chance to earn a living and to become working people living by their own labour, so long as they did not rebel or create trouble; and

that the proletariat and its party must fulfil two conditions in order to exercise leadership over their allies: (a) Lead their followers in waging resolute struggles against the common enemy and achieving victories; (b) Bring material benefits to their followers or at least avoid damaging their interests and at the same time give them political education.

These ideas of Comrade Mao Zedong's concerning policy and tactics are embodied in many of his writings, particularly in such works as *Current Problems of Tactics in the Anti-Japanese United Front, On Policy, Conclusions on the Repulse of the Second Anti-Communist Onslaught, On Some Important Problems of the Party's Present Policy, Don't Hit Out in All Directions* and *On the Question of Whether Imperialism and All Reactionaries Are Real Tigers.*

5) On ideological and political work and cultural work. In his *On New Democracy*, Comrade Mao Zedong stated:

Any given culture (as an ideological form) is a reflection of the politics and economics of a given society, and the former in turn has a tremendous influence and effect upon the latter; economics is the base and politics the concentrated expression of economics.

In accordance with the basic view, he put forward many important ideas of far-reaching and long-term significance. For instance, the theses that ideological and political work is the life-blood of economic and all other work and that it is necessary to unite politics and economics and to unite politics and professional skills, and to be both red and expert; the policy of developing a national, scientific and mass culture and of letting a hundred flowers blossom, weeding through the old to bring forth the new, and making the past serve the present and foreign things serve China; and the thesis that intellectuals have an important role to play in revolution and construction, that intellectuals should identify themselves with the workers and peasants and that they should acquire the proletarian world outlook by studying Marxism-Leninism, by studying society and through practical work. He pointed out that "this question of 'for whom?' is fundamental; it is a question of principle" and stressed that we should serve the people wholeheartedly, be highly responsible in revolutionary work, wage arduous struggle and fear no sacrifice. Many notable works written by Comrade Mao Zedong on ideology, politics and culture, such as *The Orientation of the Youth Movement, Recruit Large Numbers of Intellectuals, Talks at the Yanan Forum of Literature and Art, In Memory of Norman Bethune, Serve the People* and *The Foolish Old Man Who Removed the Mountains*, are of tremendous significance even today.

6) On Party building. It was a most difficult task to build a Marxist, proletarian Party of a mass character in a country where the peasantry and other sections of the petty bourgeoisie constituted the majority of the population, while the proletariat was small in number yet strong in combat effectiveness. Comrade Mao Zedong's theory on Party building provided a successful solution to this question. His main works in this area include *Combat Liberalism, The Role of the Chinese Communist Party in the National War, Reform Our Study, Rectify the Party's Style of Work, Oppose Stereotyped Party Writing, Our Study and the Current Situation, On Strengthening the Party Committee System and Methods of Work of Party Committees.* He laid particular stress on building the Party ideologically, saying that a Party member should join the Party not only organizationally but also ideologically and should constantly try to reform his non-proletarian ideas and replace them with proletarian ideas. He indicated that the style of work which entailed integrating theory with practice, forging close links with the masses and practising self-criticism was the hallmark distinguishing the Chinese Communist Party from all other political parties in China. To counter the erroneous "Left" policy of "ruthless struggle and merciless blows" once followed in inner-Party struggle, he proposed the correct policy of "learning from past mistakes to avoid future ones and curing the sickness to save the patient," emphasizing the need to achieve the objective of clarity in ideology and unity among comrades in inner-Party struggle. He initiated the rectification campaign as a form of ideological education in Marxism-Leninism throughout the Party, which applied the method of criticism and self-criticism. In view of the fact that our Party was about to become and then became a party in power leading the whole country, Comrade Mao Zedong urged time

and again, first on the eve of the founding of the People's Republic and then later, that we should remain modest and prudent, guard against arrogance and rashness and keep to plain living and hard struggle in our style of work and that we should be on the lookout against the corrosive influence of bourgeois ideology and should oppose bureaucratism which would alienate us from the masses.

30. The living soul of Mao Zedong Thought is the stand, viewpoint and method embodied in its component parts mentioned above. This stand, viewpoint and method boil down to three basic points: to seek truth from facts, the mass line, and independence. Comrade Mao Zedong applied dialectical and historical materialism to the entire work of the proletarian party, giving shape to this stand, viewpoint and method so characteristic of Chinese Communists in the course of the Chinese revolution and its arduous, protracted struggles and thus enriching Marxism-Leninism. They find expression not only in such important works as *Oppose Book Worship, On Practice, On Contradiction, Preface and Postscript to "Rural Surveys," Some Questions Concerning Methods of Leadership* and *Where Do Correct Ideas Come Form?*, but also in all his scientific writings and in the revolutionary activities of the Chinese Communists.

1) Seeking truth from facts. This means proceeding from reality and combining theory with practice, that is, integrating the universal principles of Marxism-Leninism with the concrete practice of the Chinese revolution. Comrade Mao Zedong was always against studying Marxism in isolation from the realities of Chinese society and the Chinese revolution. As early as 1930, he opposed blind book worship by emphasizing that investigation and study is the first step in all work and that one has no right to speak without investigation. On the eve of the rectification movement in Yanan, he affirmed that subjectivism is a formidable enemy of the Communist Party, a manifestation of impurity in Party spirit. These brilliant theses helped people break through the shackles of dogmatism and greatly emancipate their minds. While summarizing the experience and lessons of the Chinese revolution in his philosophical works and many other works rich in philosophical content, Comrade Mao Zedong showed great profundity in expounding and enriching the Marxist theory of knowledge and dialectics. He stressed that the dialectical materialist theory of knowledge is the dynamic, revolutionary theory of reflection and that full scope should be given to man's conscious dynamic role which is based on and is in conformity with objective reality. Basing himself on social practice, he comprehensively and systematically elaborated the dialectical materialist theory on the sources, the process and the purpose of knowledge and on the criterion of truth. He said that as a rule, correct

knowledge can be arrived at and developed only after many repetitions of the process leading from matter to consciousness and then back to matter, that is, leading from practice to knowledge and then back to practice. He pointed out that truth exists by contrast with falsehood and grows in struggle with it, that truth is inexhaustible and that the truth of any piece of knowledge, namely, whether it corresponds to objective reality, can ultimately be decided only through social practice. He further elaborated the law of the unity of opposites, the nucleus of Marxist dialectics. He indicated that we should not only study the universality of contradiction in objective existence, but, what is more important, we should study the particularity of contradiction, and that we should resolve contradictions which are different in nature by different methods. Therefore, dialectics should not be viewed as a formula to be learnt by rote and applied mechanically, but should be closely linked with practice and with investigation and study and should be applied flexibly. He forged philosophy into a sharp weapon in the hands of the proletariat and the people for knowing and changing the world. His distinguished works on China's revolutionary war, in particular, provide outstandingly shining examples of applying and developing the Marxist theory of knowledge and dialectics in practice. Our Party must always adhere to the above ideological line formulated by Comrade Mao Zedong.

2) The mass line means everything for the masses, reliance on the masses in everything and "from the masses, to the masses." The Party's mass line in all its work has come into being through the systematic application in all its activities of the Marxist-Leninist principle that the people are the makers of history. It is a summation of our Party's invaluable historical experience in conducting revolutionary activities over the years under difficult circumstances in which the enemy's strength far outstripped ours. Comrade Mao Zedong stressed time and again that as long as we rely on the people, believe firmly in the inexhaustible creative power of the masses and hence trust and identify ourselves with them, no enemy can crush us while we can eventually crush every enemy and overcome every difficulty. He also pointed out that in leading the masses in all practical work, the leadership can form its correct ideas only by adopting the method of "from the masses, to the masses" and by combining the leadership with the masses and combining the general call with particular guidance. This means concentrating the ideas of the masses and turning them into systematic ideas, then going to the masses so that the ideas are persevered in and carried through, and testing the correctness of these ideas in the practice of the masses. And this process goes on, over and over again, so that the understanding of the leadership becomes more correct, keener and richer each time. This is how Comrade Mao Zedong united the

Marxist theory of knowledge with the Party's mass line. As the vanguard of the proletariat, the Party exists and fights for the interests of the people. But it always constitutes only a small part of the people, so that isolation from the people will render all the Party's struggles and ideals devoid of content as well as impossible of success. To persevere in the revolution and advance the socialist cause, our Party must uphold the mass line.

3) Independence and self-reliance are the inevitable corollary of carrying out the Chinese revolution and construction by proceeding from Chinese reality and relying on the masses. The proletarian revolution is an internationalist cause which calls for the mutual support of the proletariats of different countries. But for the cause to triumph, each proletariat should primarily base itself on its own country's realities, rely on the efforts of its own masses and revolutionary forces, integrate the universal principles of Marxism-Leninism with the concrete practice of its own revolution and thus achieve victory. Comrade Mao Zedong always stressed that our policy should rest on our own strength and that we should find our own road of advance in accordance with our own conditions. In a vast country like China, we must all the more rely mainly on our own efforts to promote the revolution and construction. We must be determined to carry the struggle through to the end and must have faith in the hundreds of millions of Chinese people and rely on their wisdom and strength; otherwise, it will be impossible for our revolution and construction to succeed or to be consolidated even if success is won. Of course, China's revolution and national construction are not and cannot be carried on in isolation from the rest of the world. It is always necessary for us to try to win foreign aid and, in particular, to learn all that is advanced and beneficial from other countries. The closed-door policy, blind opposition to everything foreign and any theory or practice of great-nation chauvinism are all entirely wrong. At the same time, although China is still comparatively backward economically and culturally, we must maintain our own national dignity and confidence and there must be no slavishness or submissiveness in any form in dealing with big, powerful or rich countries. Under the leadership of the Party and Comrade Mao Zedong, no matter what difficulty we encountered, we never wavered, whether before or after the founding of New China, in our determination to remain independent and self-reliant and we never submitted to any pressure from outside; we showed the dauntless and heroic spirit of the Chinese Communist Party and the Chinese people. We stand for the peaceful coexistence of the people of all countries and their mutual assistance on an equal footing. While upholding our own independence, we respect other people's right to independence. The road of revolution and construction suited to the characteristics of a country has to be explored,

decided on and blazed by its own people. No one has the right to impose his views on others. Only under these conditions can there be genuine internationalism. Otherwise, there can only be hegemonism. We will always adhere to this principled stand in our international relations.

31. Mao Zedong Thought is the valuable spiritual asset of our Party. It will be our guide to action for a long time to come. The Party leaders and the large group of cadres nurtured by Marxism-Leninism and Mao Zedong Thought were the backbone forces in winning great victories for our cause; they are and will remain our treasured mainstay in the cause of socialist modernization. While many of Comrade Mao Zedong's important works were written during the periods of new-democratic revolution and of socialist transformation, we must still constantly study them. This is not only because one cannot cut the past off from the present and failure to understand the past will hamper our understanding of present-day problems, but also because many of the basic theories, principles and scientific approaches set forth in these works are of universal significance and provide us with invaluable guidance now and will continue to do so in the future. Therefore, we must continue to uphold Mao Zedong Thought, study it in earnest and apply its stand, viewpoint and method in studying the new situation and solving the new problems arising in the course of practice. Mao Zedong Thought has added much that is new to the treasure-house of Marxist-Leninist theory. We must combine our study of the scientific works of Comrade Mao Zedong with that of the scientific writings of Marx, Engels, Lenin and Stalin. It is entirely wrong to try to negate the scientific value of Mao Zedong Thought and to deny its guiding role in our revolution and construction just because Comrade Mao Zedong made mistakes in his later years. And it is likewise entirely wrong to adopt a dogmatic attitude towards the sayings of Comrade Mao Zedong to regard whatever he said as the immutable truth which must be mechanically applied everywhere, and to be unwilling to admit honestly that he made mistakes in his later years, and even try to stick to them in our new activities. Both these attitudes fail to make a distinction between the Mao Zedong Thought—a scientific theory formed and tested over a long period of time—and the mistakes Comrade Mao Zedong made in his later years. And it is absolutely necessary that this distinction should be made. We must treasure all the positive experience obtained in the course of integrating the universal principles of Marxism-Leninism with the concrete practice of China's revolution and construction over 50 years or so, apply and carry forward this experience in our new work, enrich and develop Party theory with new principles and new conclusions corresponding to reality, so as to ensure the continued progress of our cause along the scientific course of Marxism-Leninism and Mao Zedong Thought.

Publications of Prof. Stuart R. Schram

I. On China

A. BOOKS

Mao Zedong, *Une étude de l'éducation physique* (translation, with an introduction). Paris: Mouton, 1962, 66 pp. + Chinese text

Documents sur la théorie de la "révolution permanente" en Chine. Idéologie dialectique et dialectique du réel (translation, with an introduction). Paris: Mouton, 1963, xlix + 65 pp.

The Political Thought of Mao Tse-tung. New York: Praeger, 1963; revised edition, 1969, 479 pp.

Mao Tse-tung, *Basic Tactics* (translation, with an introduction). New York: Praeger, 1966, 149 pp.

Mao Tse-tung. Harmondsworth: Penguin, 1966; revised edition, 1967, 372 pp. (Also published in hardback in the U. S. by Simon and Schuster.)

Quotations from Chairman Mao (edited, with an introduction). New York: Bantam Books, 1967, xxx + 182 pp.

Marxism and Asia (in collaboration with Hélène Carrère d'Encausse) London: Allen Lane the Penguin Press, 1969, 404 pp. (Revised and expanded edition of a work originally published in French in 1965.)

L'U.R.S.S. et la Chine devant les révolutions dans les sociétés pré-industrielles (with Hélène Carrère d'Encausse). Paris: Armand Colin, 1970, 108 pp.

Authority, Participation, and Cultural Change in China (edited, with an extended introduction). Cambridge: Cambridge University Press, 1973, 350 pp.

Mao Tse-tung Unrehearsed. Talks and Letters 1956-1971 (edited, and with an introduction). Harmondsworth: Penguin, 1974, 352 pp. (Also published in the U. S. by Pantheon under the title *Chairman Mao Talks to the People*.)

(NOTE: The above list does not include translations. *Mao Tse-tung* has been translated into ten languages; *The Political Thought of Mao Tse-tung*, *Marxism and Asia*, and *Mao Tse-tung Unrehearsed* have each appeared in four or five languages.)

B. ARTICLES

"Chinese and Leninist Components in the Personality of Mao Tse-tung," *Asian Survey* III(6), 1963, pp. 259-273.

"The 'Military Deviation' of Mao Tse-tung," *Problems of Communism* no. 1, 1964, pp. 49-56.

"On the Nature of Mao Tse-tung's 'Deviation' in 1927," *The China Quarterly* no. 18, 1964, pp. 55-66.

"Mao as a Poet," *Problems of Communism* no. 5, 1964, pp. 38-44.

"La Chine de Mao Tsé-toung," *Revue française de science politique* no. 6, 1965, pp. 1079-1110.

"Mao: the Man and his Doctrines," contribution to a symposium in *Problems of Communism* no. 5, 1966, pp. 1-7.

"Mao Tse-tung and Secret Societies," *The China Quarterly* no. 27, 1966, pp. 1-13.

"Mao as a Charismatic Leader," *Asian Survey* VII(6), 1967, pp. 383-388.

"Mao Tse-tung and the Chinese Political Equilibrium," *Government and Opposition* IV(1), 1969, pp. 141-158.

"Mao Tse-tung and the Search for a 'Chinese Road' to Socialism," *Royal Central Asian Journal* LVI(1), 1969, pp. 30-41.

"The Party in Chinese Communist Ideology," in J. W. Lewis (ed.), *Party Leadership and Revolutionary Power in China* (Cambridge: Cambridge University Press, 1970), pp. 170-202.

"Mao Tse-tung and the Theory of the Permanent Revolution, 1958-1969," *The China Quarterly* no. 46, 1971, pp. 221-244.

"Social Revolution and Cultural Revolution in China," in A. Dyson and B. Towers (eds.), *China and the West: Mankind Evolving* (London: Garnstone Press, 1970), pp. 65-81.

"Mō Takutō shisō ni okeru Reninshugi to jinminshugi" (Leninism and Populism in the Thought of Mao Tse-tung), *Ajichō Geppō* no. 1, 1970, pp. 2-22.

"Mao Tse-tung and Liu Shao-ch'i, 1939-1969," *Asian Survey* XII(4), 1972, pp. 275-293.

"Mō Takutō no tai-So taido (1958-1962 nen)" (Mao Tse-tung's Attitude toward the Soviets, 1958-1962), *The Asia Quarterly* (Tokyo) III(3), 1971, pp. 2-23.

"Mao Tse-tung Gestern und Heute," in F. A. Lutz (ed.), *Ostasien: Tradition und Umbruch* (Zürich: Rentsch Verlag, 1971), pp. 85-113.

"Mao and Maoism," in J. M. Gibson and D. M. Johnson (eds.), *A Century of Struggle: Canadian Essays on Revolutionary China* (Toronto: Canadian Institute of International Affairs, 1971), pp. 118-132.

"From the 'Great Union of the Popular Masses' to the 'Great Alliance'" (preceded by a translation of Mao Tse-tung, "The Great Union of the Popular Masses"), *The China Quarterly* no. 49, 1972, pp. 76-105.

"Some Recent Studies of Revolutionary Movements in China in the Early Twentieth Century," *Bulletin of the School of Oriental and African Studies* XXXV(3), 1972, pp. 588-605.

"Mao Zedong and the Role of the Various Classes in the Chinese Revolution, 1923-1927," in *Chūgoku no seiji to keizai/The Polity and Economy of China* (The Late Professor Yuji Muramatsu Commemoration Volume) (Tokyo: Tōyō Keizai Shinpōsha, 1975), pp. 227-239.

"Mao Tse-tung: a Self-portrait," *The China Quarterly* no. 57, 1974, pp. 156-165.

"The Marxist," in Dick Wilson (ed.), *Mao Tse-tung in the Scales of History* (Cambridge: Cambridge University Press, 1977), pp. 35-69.

"Introduction" to Li Jui, *The Early Revolutionary Activities of Mao Tse-tung* (White Plains, N. Y.: M. E. Sharpe, 1977), pp. ix-xliii.

"Some Reflections on the Pfeffer-Walder 'Revolution' in China Studies," *Modern China* III(2), 1977, pp. 169-184.

"Chairman Hua Edits Mao's Literary Heritage: 'On the Ten Great Relationships'," *The China Quarterly* no. 69, 1977, pp. 125-135.

"Mao Tse-tung and the Soviets," *Il Politico* XLIII(3), 1977, pp. 445-464.

"Démocratie et centralisme dans la Chine d'après-Mao," *Pouvoirs* no. 3, 1977, pp. 59-70.

"Chūgoku genseiken to Mō Takutō no Isan" (The Present Régime in China and the Heritage of Mao Zedong), *Ajia Jihō* 2, 1979, pp. 9-28.

"Modernization and the Maoist Vision," *Bulletin* (International House of Japan) 36, 1979, pp. 1-22.

"Mao Zedong," *History Today* Vol. 31, April 1981, pp. 22-29.

"To Utopia and Back: a Cycle in the History of the Chinese Communist Party," *The China Quarterly* no. 87, September 1981, pp. 407-439.

"The Chinese Soviet Republic: Some Introductory Reflections," in W. E. Butler (ed.), *The Legal System of the Chinese Soviet Republic* (Dobbs Ferry, N. Y.: Transnational Publishers, 1983), pp. 7-20.

"Mao Tse-tung," in Tom Bottomore (ed.), *A Dictionary of Marxist Thought* (Oxford: Basil Blackwell; and Cambridge, Mass.: Harvard University Press, 1983).

"Classes, Old and New, in Mao Zedong's Thought, 1949-1976," in J. L. Watson (ed.), *Class and Social Stratification in Post-Revolution China* (Cambridge: Cambridge University Press, forthcoming).

"Decentralization in a Unitary State: Theory and Practice, 1940-1983," in S. Schram (ed.), *The State in China*, Vol. 1 (forthcoming).

C. UNPUBLISHED CONFERENCE PAPERS

"The Uses of Political Power: Mao Tse-tung's Approach in the Light of the Confucian, Legalist and Taoist Traditions" (Prepared for the Annual Meeting of the Conference for the Study of Political Thought, Toronto, April 1977.) (Documentary Background Paper, 21 pp., + Oral Presentation, 31 pp., mimeographed.)

II. On other topics (a brief, selective list)

A. BOOK

Protestantism and Politics in France. Alençon, 1954. (Doctoral thesis, privately printed, sold through book dealers in Paris and Oxford.)

B. ARTICLES

"Le poujadisme dans le Gard," *Christianisme social* nos. 3-4, 1956.

"L'Union soviétique et les Etats baltes," in J.-B. Duroselle (ed.), *Les frontières européennes de l'U.R.S.S.* (Paris: Armand Colin, 1957), pp. 25-166.

"Le protestantisme rural: traditions, structures, et tendances politiques" (in collaboration with Pierre Poujol), in H. Mendras (ed.), *Les paysans et la politique* (Paris: Armand Colin, 1958), pp. 361-385.

"Christian Rakovskij et le premier rapprochement franco-soviétique," *Cahiers du monde russe et soviétique* no. 2, 1960, and no. 4, 1961, pp. 205-237 and 584-629. (This article is a fragment of a larger work, on Franco-Soviet relations 1924-1941, which was completed in draft form but never published because of certain problems regarding use of materials from the French archives.)